W9-BRD-426

Kazakhstan's Nuclear Disarmament

A Global Model for a Safer World

Washington, DC
2006

8/07   Gift - Pub.

"The threat of nuclear terrorism puts us in a race between cooperation and catastrophe. The kind of cooperation we see again and again from Kazakhstan on a continuing basis can help us win that race."

Sam Nunn
Co-chairman and
Chief Executive Officer,
Nuclear Threat Initiative
Former U.S. Senator (D-GA)

This book is published jointly by the
Embassy of the Republic of Kazakhstan to the United States of America
and the Nuclear Threat Initiative.

Embassy of Kazakhstan
1401 16th Street, NW
Washington, DC 20036
Tel. 202 232 5488
Fax 202 232 5845
www.kazakhembus.com

Nuclear Threat Initiative
1747 Pennsylvania Avenue, NW, 7th Floor
Washington, DC 20006
Tel. 202 296 4810
Fax 202 296 4811
www.nti.org

ISBN 1-4243-1506-9

*To courage, vision and unwavering commitment of
all those who treasure peace...*

Contents

Foreword

The end of the Cold War seemed to offer the promise of a more peaceful world, without the threat of a nation-ending nuclear exchange between the two superpowers. But at the same time Cold War dangers receded, new nuclear dangers began emerging, with nations pursuing nuclear weapons programs and the very real possibility that terrorists could acquire and use nuclear weapons. In 1998, both Pakistan and India tested nuclear weapons and became nuclear weapons states. North Korea has withdrawn from the Nuclear Nonproliferation Treaty and is believed to be producing nuclear weapons. The international community continues to have questions and tensions about the nuclear program of Iran and its real direction. Moreover, both the United States and Russia, the world's two largest nuclear powers, continue to maintain thousands of nuclear weapons on hair trigger alert which today increases the risk of an accidental nuclear exchange.

Against this background, it is critical to recognize, support and emulate the efforts of those who are working to prevent a nuclear nightmare. Among the leaders, Kazakhstan must be recognized for its exemplary contributions over many years to preventing the spread and use of nuclear weapons.

Kazakhstan's leadership began in 1991 when President Nursultan Nazarbayev made the courageous decision to shut down the world's second largest nuclear test site at Semipalatinsk. After Kazakhstan regained its independence, in 1994, President Nazarbayev went a step further and, in partnership with the United States under the Nunn-Lugar program, renounced the nuclear weapons in Kazakhstan, leading to decisions by Ukraine and Belarus to renounce the weapons located in those nations as well. At the time, Kazakhstan had in excess of 1,400 nuclear weapons on its territory, more than France's, Great Britain's and China's nuclear capabilities combined. Kazakhstan's actions are a model for the kind of leadership and multilateral cooperation that is essential to reducing global nuclear dangers.

Kazakhstan continues to play a leading role. In a joint project between the Nuclear Threat Initiative (NTI) and Kazatomprom, Kazakhstan's national nuclear company, announced in 2005, up to two dozen bombs worth of nuclear weapons-usable material was successfully removed from a closing power reactor site on the Caspian Sea to Ust-Kamenogorsk, where it was blended into safe, non-weapon-usable forms of uranium. This project can be a model for other countries as a way to prevent adversaries and terrorists from acquiring nuclear weapons.

This initiative was celebrated at "Kazakhstan: Strengthening International Cooperation for Peace and Security," a symposium that took place in Ust-Kamenogorsk in October 2005. The conference was attended by President Nazarbayev, U.S. Undersecretary of State for Arms Control and International Security Robert Joseph, NTI Co-chairmen Sam Nunn and Ted Turner, President of NATO's Parliamentary Assembly Pierre Lellouche, and a number of diplomats, experts and journalists from countries throughout the world. U.S President George W. Bush and IAEA Director General Mohammed ElBaradei sent congratulatory messages to symposium participants.

This book explores the NTI-Kazatomprom project and its significance for reducing nuclear dangers. It includes speeches from the symposium, a detailed history of the project and related news articles. The book also explains the history and related circumstances that influenced Kazakhstan's ultimate decision to abandon its nuclear program.

Since independence, Kazakhstan has sought to move its citizens away from the dangers and the suffering that were caused by the Soviet Union conducting nuclear tests at Semipalatinsk during the Cold War by consistently opposing the creation, testing and deployment of nuclear, biological and chemical weapons. After 15 years of robust commitment to the global nonproliferation regime, Kazakhstan has become recognized as a reliable and solid partner which has achieved significant successes in social, economic and political development.

Today, as we face the threat of more nations and terrorist groups acquiring nuclear weapons, both the actions and the continued leadership in the nuclear nonproliferation field that we see from Kazakhstan stand as models for the cooperation that is imperative in the 21st century.

<table>
<tr><td>Kanat Saudabayev
Ambassador of the
Republic of Kazakhstan
to the United States of
America</td><td>Sam Nunn
Co-chairman and
Chief Executive Officer,
Nuclear Threat Initiative,
Former U.S. Senator (D-GA)</td></tr>
</table>

Chapter 1

Kazakhstan-Nuclear Threat Initiative Highly Enriched Uranium Down-Blending Project:

An Example for the World

Kazakhstan: Strengthening International Cooperation for Peace and Security

An International Symposium

Co-organized by
The Embassy of the Republic of Kazakhstan to the United
States of America, Nuclear Threat Initiative and
The Nonproliferation Support Center

Ust-Kamenogorsk, Kazakhstan, October 8, 2005

Nursultan Nazarbayev
President of the Republic of Kazakhstan

Robert Joseph
United States Under Secretary of State for
Arms Control and International Security

Ted Turner
Co-chairman, Nuclear Threat Initiative

Kassymzhomart Tokaev
Minister of Foreign Affairs of Kazakhstan

Pierre Lellouche
Deputy of the French National Assembly,
President of the NATO Parliamentary Assembly

Kenji Murakami
Director of Safeguards
Division of Inspections in the Department of Safeguards,
The International Atomic Energy Agency (IAEA)

Vladimir Shkolnik
Minister of Energy and Mineral Resources of Kazakhstan

Susan Eisenhower
President Emeritus, The Eisenhower Institute

Kanat Saudabayev
Ambassador Extraordinary and Plenipotentiary of the
Republic of Kazakhstan to the United States of America

Sam Nunn
Co-chairman and Chief Executive Officer,
Nuclear Threat Initiative.
Former U.S. Senator (D-GA)

3

President Nursultan Nazarbayev

Nursultan Nazarbayev:

People of Kazakhstan Stand By Our Historic Non-Nuclear-Weapons Choice and Call on Other Countries to Follow Us

I am happy to greet this distinguished audience on the hospitable land of Kazakhstan. Our republic, especially its eastern region where we are today, has immediate relevance to the theme of this international symposium. That this event is taking place here is recognition of the important role Kazakhstan has played in the process of nonproliferation, in the struggle for security and for sustainable economic development.

Earlier today you had the opportunity to visit atomic energy facilities in Ust-Kamenogorsk. Not far from here, near Semipalatinsk, one of the world's largest nuclear test sites had operated until recently.

During the half century of the test site's existence, more than 450 nuclear and thermonuclear explosions were carried out there. That is why like few other peoples, the people of Kazakhstan know the horrible consequences of nuclear testing. Today, not only the unwilling witnesses of those explosions but their children and grandchildren continue to suffer. That was one of the most difficult and tragic pages of Kazakhstan's history.

Along with the permanent shutdown of the Semipalatinsk nuclear test site our country took the decision to renounce a deadly nuclear weapons inheritance.

After the break up of the Soviet Union, our republic inherited a considerable number of nuclear weapons including strategic missiles with multiple warheads, notoriously known in the West as 'Satan' missiles, and nuclear and thermonuclear warheads for these missiles. At that moment, this deadly arsenal was the fourth largest in the world.

Kazakhstan had 148 silos for land based intercontinental ballistic missiles (ICBMs). These silos held 104 ICBMs with

5

nuclear warheads. The load of these missiles was 7.6 metric tons; each capable of flying 12,000 kilometers.

For the first time in the history of the world, our country, Kazakhstan, made the decision to voluntarily renounce these terrifying arms. This was our conscious choice dictated primarily by the fact that the people of Kazakhstan had personal knowledge of the ghastly consequences of nuclear weapons testing.

The decision to renounce our nuclear arsenal laid the foundation for Kazakhstan's overall strategy for global security.

The countries of the "nuclear club" supported us. The United States of America, Russia and the United Kingdom, under an agreement signed by the presidents of those countries in Budapest on December 5, 1994, provided guarantees of security and territorial integrity for Kazakhstan in response to our renunciation of nuclear weapons. China and France later provided similar guarantees.

Figuratively speaking, from that moment Kazakhstan became an 'epicenter of peace', a place where for the first time in history people who had possessed a destructive force voluntarily renounced it. As you would recall, a few years ago I wrote a book called *Epicenter of Peace*.

By that decision, we proved in practice our desire to live in peace, friendship and good neighborliness with all the countries and peoples of the world. I believe this can be considered an independent Kazakhstan's contribution to strengthening the stability and security of the planet.

On the other hand, Kazakhstan has managed to attract large investments in our economy and gained the opportunity to use all available resources to raise our citizens' wellbeing. Today, our country is a leader in economic and political reforms in the post Soviet area. Our rates of economic growth, at nine to ten percent annually on average, are considered among the highest in the world.

Kazakhstan has become a firm advocate of disarmament and of the fight against extremism and international terrorism.

Today, one of the key elements for stability of the modern world is a sustainable system of global security.

The high level of modern science and technologies, available databases of information across an entire spectrum of knowledge, and the falling cost of industrial technologies should have been put to use solely for the good of mankind. Unfortunately, progress opens new opportunities not only for peaceful development, but also for opposing progress. That is why the global security system should be continuously improved and should accompany technological developments.

Stringent control over weapons, the most dangerous materials and technologies is a key element of nonproliferation and the foundation of any security system. Fighting proliferation of both weapons and their components on a global scope is an effective measure for containing terrorism and aggressive aspirations.

The largest international program to promote the nonproliferation regime is the Cooperative Threat Reduction Program, which became known from 1993 and 1995 as the Nunn-Lugar Program, after the two U.S. senators who were its authors.

The original goal of the Nunn-Lugar Program was to reduce the threat to the security of the United States but with time it has become a strategy of international cooperation for many other countries participating in it.

Every new stage of this program widens its activities, sets more complex tasks and expands the number of participants.

The activities of the Cooperative Threat Reduction Program in Kazakhstan clearly show all these qualities.

Let us recall recent historic events. In 1992, while enduring a complicated social and economic situation Kazakhstan became the world's fourth largest nuclear power following the collapse of the Soviet Union.

The temptation to keep those weapons was a great one. This was the advice of some of the 'friendly' countries. Inside the country, there were also groups of renowned people who believed the renunciation of nuclear weapons was a mistake.

However, no difficulties could influence our principled decision to proclaim Kazakhstan a non-nuclear-weapons country. This historic choice predetermined Kazakhstan's further strategies in the sphere of global security.

The main point of our foreign policies has become the development of nonproliferation regimes.

Therefore, the goals of Kazakhstan and the United States in nonproliferation and reduction of risks of use of weapons of mass destruction were similar from the early stages of the Nunn-Lugar Program.

The fall of 2000 marked a milestone in the Program's implementation. By that time, a five year program to eliminate the nuclear weapons infrastructure at the Semipalatinsk test site was completed.

Documents were signed reflecting new directions for joint activities, including preventing the proliferation of especially dangerous materials and dual use technologies. This allowed the start of the work on safe preservation of nuclear materials at Kazakhstan's BN-350 nuclear reactor and its decommissioning.

We needed to put approximately two thousand nine hundred kilograms of nuclear fuel with highly enriched uranium in conditions completely eliminating the risk of its illegal use.

In 2001, Senator Sam Nunn and Charles Curtis, President of Nuclear Threat Initiative (NTI), offered the Government of Kazakhstan assistance in solving this problem. Technical teams from both sides developed a project which became known as 'Safe transportation and downblending of highly enriched uranium contained in fresh BN-350 reactor fuel.'

The project's main objective was to 'strengthen the global security through reducing the risk of use of weapons of mass destruction.'

I am pleased to say that today the project is almost completed. Nuclear Threat Initiative provided co-financing for all stages of the project, plus monitoring and expertise for its implementation. Kazakhstan's facilities successfully achieved the tasks set before them.

To conclude, I would like to note that the main method for preventing proliferation of the most dangerous nuclear, chemical and bacteriological materials has been and remains the system of accountability, control and physical protection of these materials. In recent years, the U.S. has fully modified its security system and offered assistance to countries of the Commonwealth of Independent States in developing their own systems.

A modern security system should completely preclude the possibilities of illegal access to or proliferation of materials in emergency situations. This is the goal of NTI's projects in Kazakhstan, 'Strengthening the physical protection and preventing the proliferation of dangerous materials.'

However, wherever possible the most reliable and economically viable way to eliminate the threat of proliferation of such materials is their transformation into conditions which exclude their military use. Fast breeder reactors have been used in industrial installations for more than 40 years. This means problems which led to the project we celebrate today will appear more frequently.

The project in Kazakhstan and the successful practice of down-blending highly enriched uranium into low enriched uranium can be a successful example and a basis for similar projects and programs in other regions and countries. Kazakhstan is willing to actively share our experience and provide assistance and participate in implementing such projects.

We hope our example will be positive for other countries. In recent years we saw as agreements within the UN framework aimed at nuclear containment, nonproliferation and non-production of nuclear materials were not successful. Our neighbors, Pakistan and India, became nuclear powers. This means the world needs to adopt a completely different solution from its current one. Saying that nuclear weapons must not be developed by other countries and must not be proliferated, the nuclear powers themselves, especially the largest ones such as the United States, Russia and others, should make an example by reducing their own arsenals.

According to existing agreements in the world today some are allowed to have weapons and even modernize them, while others are forbidden from having them or even developing them. That is incorrect, disproportionate and unfair. Within the United Nations, the covenant must be reviewed with a new view for global actions and responsibility of all countries, primarily nuclear ones, in terms of reducing nuclear weapons and gradual elimination of them.

We believe the steps we took in the past decade became yet another considerable contribution to preserving stability and security in the world. The people of Kazakhstan stand by our historic non-nuclear-weapons choice and call upon other countries to follow us.

President George W. Bush

October 5, 2005

His Excellency
Nursultan Nazarbayev
President of the Republic of Kazakhstan
Astana

Dear Mr. President:

I send greetings to you and those gathered in Ust-Kamenogorsk to mark Kazakhstan's continued success in converting nuclear material to peaceful and productive uses.

Kazakhstan has been a leader in countering the threat of weapons of mass destruction. With help from the Nunn-Lugar Program, Kazakhstan has eliminated the weapons of mass destruction and related infrastructure inherited from the Soviet Union.

More remains to be done, and I look forward to continuing our two nations' cooperation to eliminate trafficking in weapons of mass destruction.

Sincerely,

George W. Bush

Robert Joseph
United States Under Secretary of State for Arms Control and International Security

 Robert Joseph serves as the Under Secretary of State for Arms Control and International Security since June 1, 2005. In this capacity, he is the principal State officer for non- and counterproliferation matters, as well as for arms control, arms transfers, regional security and defense relations, and security assistance. Previously, he served as Special Assistant to the President and Senior Director for Proliferation Strategy, Counterproliferation and Homeland Defense, National Security Council. In this position he was responsible, under the supervision of the National Security Advisor, for developing and coordinating U.S. policies and strategies for preventing and defending against threats to the United States from weapons of mass destruction.

From 1992 until 2001, Dr. Joseph was Professor of National Security Studies and Director/Founder of the Center for Counterproliferation Research at the National Defense University. Prior to that he was U.S. Commissioner to the Standing Consultative Commission and Ambassador to the U.S.-Russian Consultative Commission on Nuclear Testing, Principal Deputy Assistant Secretary of Defense for International Security Policy, and Deputy Assistant Secretary for Nuclear Forces and Arms Control Policy.

Dr. Joseph received his MA from the University of Chicago and his Ph.D. from Columbia University. He has held Assistant Professor positions at the Fletcher School of Law and Diplomacy, Tulane University, and Carleton College.

Robert Joseph:

We Should Seize the Opportunity to Cooperate More Broadly Against Global Proliferation

It is a pleasure to be in Kazakhstan and experience the warm hospitality of your great country. I am pleased to be with you today to commemorate another landmark in cooperation between the United States and Kazakhstan against the threat of weapons of mass destruction.

It is my particular privilege to present to you, Mr. President, a letter from President Bush, which underscores the importance he places on our continuing work together.

Allow me to read that letter: "Dear Mr. President, I send greetings to you and those gathered in Ust-Kamenogorsk to mark Kazakhstan's continued success in converting nuclear material to peaceful and productive uses.

Kazakhstan has been a leader in countering the threat of weapons of mass destruction. With help from the Nunn-Lugar Program, Kazakhstan has eliminated the weapons of mass destruction and related infrastructure inherited from the Soviet Union.

More remains to be done, and I look forward to continuing our two nations' cooperation to eliminate trafficking in weapons of mass destruction. Sincerely, George W. Bush".

The new down-blending facility, which we saw today, is turning fuel that was to be used to breed weapons grade plutonium, into low enriched uranium to produce electric power. It is especially fitting that this same facility was the site of one of our greatest joint accomplishments, Project Sapphire, the removal of over one-half-ton of highly enriched uranium to make it available only for peaceful nuclear fuel, and not for the deadly purposes of terrorists or those who support them.

Mr. President, you and your government demonstrated from the earliest days of independent Kazakhstan that your real strength would come not from retaining deadly arsenals, but from cooperating with the world community to reduce and counter such threats.

Mr. President, you have ended the weapons legacy which you inherited from the Soviet Union. This is an important accomplishment which we pause today to acknowledge. As we complete that work, we should seize the opportunity to cooperate more broadly against global proliferation. By transforming the facilities and expertise in your country, which once were used for weapons, you set the example for others of how to effectively transform weapons for peaceful purposes.

There is far more that we can and should do together bilaterally, with regional partners, and with the broader international community. I applaud Kazakhstan's endorsement of the Proliferation Security Initiative, which is one tool in ending the trafficking of weapons of mass destruction. I look forward to ever closer cooperation to reduce and end the traffic in weapons of mass destruction related materials and equipment, and their means of delivery. Our cooperation of the last 12 years is a solid basis on which to build future counterproliferation efforts. The future of our strong partnership has never been brighter.

President Nursultan Nazarbayev addresses the symposium in Ust-Kamenogorsk on October 8, 2005, calling on the world to learn from Kazakhstan's example of nuclear disarmament.

NTI Co-chairman Ted Turner tells his audience a "nuclear sword of Damocles" hanging over humanity must be eliminated.

Robert Joseph, U.S. Undersecretary of State for Arms Control and International Security makes a ringing call for greater cooperation against the growing threat of global proliferation of weapons of mass destruction.

The now idle BN-350 fast breeder nuclear reactor near Aktau on Kazakhstan's Caspian shore was shut down for decommissioning in 1999. The down-blended three tons of highly enriched uranium came from this reactor.

This special train carried the three tons of highly enriched uranium fuel safely across more than 4,500 kilometers from Aktau on its way to be down-blended at the Ulba plant in Ust-Kamenogorsk.

A specially trained guard watches over scores of nuclear fuel assemblies filled with highly enriched uranium brought to the Ulba plant from Aktau.

NTI Co-chairman Sam Nunn presents a crystal pyramid called "Vision" to President Nazarbayev in recognition of his "ability to look to the future and see a better path to peace."

The symposium in Ust-Kamenogorsk called on the nations of the world to follow Kazakhstan's model of nuclear disarmament and nonproliferation.

NTI Co-chairmen Sam Nunn and Ted Turner, board members and others gather around the then Minister of Energy and Mineral Resources of Kazakhstan Vladimir Shkolnik (center) as they celebrate the success of the down-blending project at the Ulba plant. Kanat Saudabayev, Kazakhstan's Ambassador to the USA, joins the group on the far right.

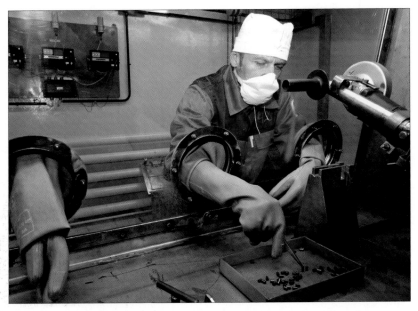

A worker carefully handles highly enriched uranium extracted from fuel assemblies in a containment chamber at UMP.

The tour group watches as an open flame is used to produce pellets of the now down-blended uranium.

Containers of newly down-blended uranium powder are stored temporarily at Ulba before being processed further.

Nurlan Mussin, UMP Director General, uses a pointer as he gives details of the sprawling plant site and its sophisticated operation.

Minister Shkolnik explains to symposium participants the structure of a fuel assembly as the group tours the Ulba Metallurgical Plant (UMP) Museum.

Ted Turner, Rebekah Stewart, and Ethan Wilensky-Lanford of the New York Times examine an element of a fuel assembly at the UMP Museum.

Kenji Murakami, the International Atomic Energy Agency's Director of Safeguards, as part of the Ulba tour, directs the group's attention to the IAEA's 24/7 television surveillance cameras which transmit their images to the Agency's headquarters in Vienna, Austria. These cameras are part of IAEA's system of safeguards at Ulba.

A panel of television screens, a key part of the Ulba technological control system, is operated by a plant worker.

Senator Sam Nunn gives a thumbs up sign of approval for the uranium down-blending project.

The real thing… The containers of low enriched uranium fuel pellets bound for peaceful civilian uses. A danger no more.

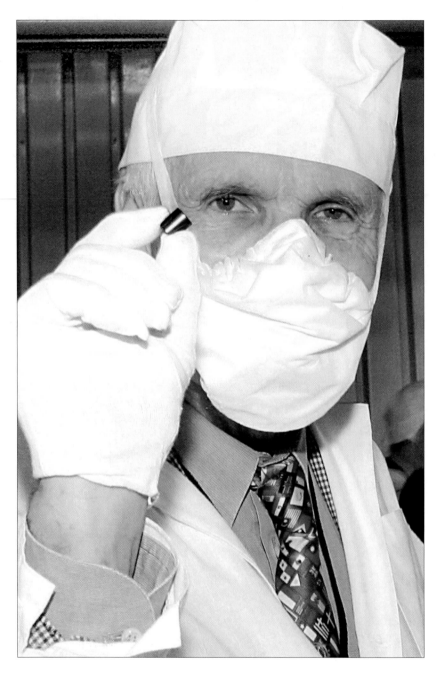

Pellets for peace... NTI's Ted Turner shows off a down-
blended low enriched uranium pellet. Mission accomplished!

Ted Turner
Co-chairman, Nuclear Threat Initiative

 Ted Turner, Co-chairman of the Nuclear Threat Initiative, is the founder of CNN, the world's first live, in-depth, around-the-clock news television network. Mr. Turner spent nearly 30 years building Turner Broadcasting System into one of the nation's largest media conglomerates. The company merged with Time Warner in 1996.

Mr. Turner began his career as an account executive for Turner Advertising Company, later to become Turner Broadcasting System. He bought his first television station in 1970 and later purchased Major League Baseball's Atlanta Braves. Mr. Turner pioneered the "superstation" concept, transmitting a station's signal to cable systems nationwide via satellite.

He founded the cable channels TNT, Cartoon Network and Turner Classic Movies, a 24-hour commercial-free network. He expanded Turner Broadcasting's news division with the creation of CNNRadio, CNN Airport Network and a 24-hour sports network.

A philanthropist and supporter of a number of humanitarian causes, Mr. Turner founded the United Nations Foundation and the Goodwill Games, an international, world class, quadrennial, multi-sport competition.

Mr. Turner is the recipient of numerous honorary degrees, industry awards and civic honors, including being named *Time* magazine's 1991 Man of the Year and one of two Men of the Century by *Broadcasting & Cable Magazine* in 1999.

Ted Turner:

It Is an Honor and Privilege to Have Been a Small Part of Your Program to Make Your Country and the World Safer

Thank you, Mr. President, for that incredible, inspiring and forward looking speech that you just gave. I could not agree with you more wholeheartedly. We are also very appreciative of the United States' support for your very courageous and intelligent decision.

It is an honor and privilege for me to be here today and to have been a small part of your program to make your country and the world safer from these horrible weapons that have hung like the sword of Damocles over humanity for the past 55 or so years.

I too have been very concerned about the existence of these thousands of weapons and encourage the large countries that have large arsenals, mainly the United States and Russia, to reduce those arsenals as much as possible and to certainly get them of hair trigger alert.

As everyone knows, the U.S. and Russian nuclear forces are still on hair trigger alert 15 years after the Cold War. It is a very complex situation. But the only reason the United States has their nuclear forces on hair trigger alert is Russia has theirs on hair trigger alert. And the only reason Russia has their nuclear forces on hair trigger alert is because the United States has theirs. It's crazy, but it is a complex issue.

The military minds in both countries, if they are given a chance, I think can come up with a formula that would give the leaders of both countries adequate time and also reduce the chances of an accident. An accident could occur with these arsenals. If it does, if there's a war with those two arsenals, it will be the end of mankind. It is really not fair for everybody to kill everybody because two countries can't figure out how to work out a solution to a not insurmountable problem.

Kassymzhomart Tokaev
Minister of Foreign Affairs of the Republic of Kazakhstan

Kassymzhomart Tokaev was appointed Minister of Foreign Affairs of the Republic of Kazakhstan in June 2003. Prior to that he served as Secretary of State and Minister of Foreign Affairs from January 2002.

From 1999 through 2002, Kassymzhomart Tokaev served as Kazakhstan's Prime Minister overseeing the beginning of the rapid economic growth Kazakhstan has enjoyed since 2000.

Minister Tokaev served as Deputy Prime Minister, Minister of Foreign Affairs from March to October 1999 and was in charge of international political and economic cooperation, attracting foreign investment, relations with the CIS countries and export control. Before that he was Kazakhstan's Minister of Foreign Affairs from October 1994 to March 1999. In 1992-94, he worked as Kazakhstan's Deputy Foreign Minister and First Deputy Foreign Minister.

From 1975 through 1992, Kassymzhomart Tokaev served at the Soviet embassies in Singapore and China, the Soviet Ministry of Foreign Affairs in Moscow, and earned diplomas from the Beijing Linguistic Institute and the Diplomatic Academy of Russia's Ministry of Foreign Affairs.

Minister Tokaev graduated from the Moscow State Institute of International Relations and has a Ph.D. in History. He holds the diplomatic rank of Ambassador Extraordinary and Plenipotentiary and is fluent in English, Chinese and French.

He has authored a number of books, including *How It Was: Chronicles of Disturbances in China (April-June 1989)* (1993), *United Nations: 50 Years of Service to Peace* (1995), *Under the Flag of Independence (Historic essays on Kazakhstan's foreign policy)* (1997), *"Foreign Policy of Kazakhstan in the Process of Globalization"* (2000), and *"Meeting the Challenge"* (2003).

19

Kassymzhomart Tokaev has been awarded the Orders of Parasat and Astana.

He was born in Almaty in 1953.

Serious Crisis in Global Security System, International Agreements Must Reflect New Reality

It is a great honor and privilege for me to address this distinguished audience and welcome you all to Ust-Kamenogorsk.

The name of this conference speaks for itself serving as recognition of Kazakhstan's valuable role in promoting global peace and security.

As you are aware, strengthening of the nonproliferation regime and continuation of the disarmament process is of paramount importance for Kazakhstan. From the very outset of our independence, Kazakhstan has been committed to a safer world free of tensions and threats and, certainly, of weapons of mass destruction. Our country has been pursuing a principled policy of demilitarization and nuclear disarmament.

The people of Kazakhstan, having personally seen the destructive force of nuclear weapons, resolutely opted to end the testing of these lethal devices. In 1991, President Nursultan Nazarbayev, expressing the wish of our people, made a decision to shut down the Semipalatinsk nuclear test site forever.

As the next step in our drive for a safer and more secure world, Kazakhstan's President took a crucial decision to renounce unilaterally the nuclear arsenal inherited from the former Soviet Union. It was indeed a courageous step by a newly independent nation.

In theory, Kazakhstan could have emerged as one of the world's nuclear superpowers. Had we taken control of the more than 1,400 nuclear warheads left on our territory when the Soviet Union disappeared, we would have commanded an arsenal larger than those of the United Kingdom, France, and China combined. Most of these warheads were deployed on missiles aimed at targets in the United States.

Kazakhstan's voluntary renunciation of our nuclear legacy and firm adherence to the nonproliferation regime predetermined our accession to the Treaty on the Nonproliferation of Nuclear Weapons (NPT) and the Comprehensive Nuclear Test Ban Treaty (CTBT).

Kazakhstan has been firmly committed to nuclear disarmament and is signatory of the Lisbon Protocol, confirming our non-nuclear-weapons status and our accession to the NPT. Another example of Kazakhstan's commitment to the nonproliferation regime was the shipment of 600 kilograms of highly enriched uranium to the United States under the International Atomic Energy Agency (IAEA) safeguards in 1994.

In 2002, Kazakhstan was accepted into the Nuclear Suppliers Group, and is now getting ready to join the Missile Technology Control Regime. Attaching great importance to the full implementation of the IAEA safeguards and to the strengthening of the Agency's verification mechanisms, Kazakhstan signed the Additional Protocol in 2004 and closely cooperates with the IAEA in this area. Kazakhstan implements additional measures to strengthen the regime for the verification of nuclear activities.

Kazakhstan's role in the former Soviet Union's nuclear missile launch capacity and weapons grade nuclear fuel production made it one of the first countries included under the Nunn-Lugar Cooperative Threat Reduction Program.

Today, as the spread of nuclear weapons takes new forms, Kazakhstan is expanding our cooperation with the United States through the Proliferation Security Initiative (PSI). The PSI will serve as a deterrent to would-be proliferators, and ensure Kazakhstan's participation in global efforts to stop proliferation of weapons of mass destruction.

Kazakhstan's cooperation with the United States under these programs is a benchmark.

We can proudly boast that Kazakhstan set a commendable example and made an outstanding and unique contribution to nonproliferation efforts which has become a significant factor in strengthening international security. President Bush has in fact cited Kazakhstan as a key example of how a state rids itself of weapons of mass destruction when it has the will to do it.

As a nation which voluntarily renounced its nuclear legacy, Kazakhstan is concerned by the continued proliferation of weapons of mass destruction.

Today, the global security system is in serious crisis. The Nonproliferation Treaty and the Comprehensive Nuclear Test Ban Treaty do not work in practice. The 2005 NPT Review Conference failed to set up a balanced and comprehensive mechanism to ensure strengthening of the international nonproliferation regime and complete elimination of nuclear weapons. Even more disturbing is the lack of clear recommendations on nonproliferation and disarmament in the final document of that conference.

The desire of a number of countries and some extremist groups to obtain nuclear weapons and other types of weapons of mass destruction poses a serious threat to global security.

The United Nations and its agencies should have the last word in solving the problem of nuclear nonproliferation. Lack of an effective mechanism which would impose sanctions at the highest international levels against those states found in violation of the nonproliferation regimes is a serious problem.

The existing international agreements in this area should be adapted to new realities. We can no longer accept the fact that some states are punished on mere suspicion that they might possess weapons of mass destruction, while others are constantly warned about the harmful nature of such a policy or are censured by means of a unilateral embargo, while still others are simply forgiven.

We in Kazakhstan strongly believe that there must be no bargaining on issues of nuclear nonproliferation. There must be no excuse for nuclear weapons trade. There must be no mercy for countries engaged in production or sale of nuclear weapons. There must be no differentiation between the so called 'good' and 'bad' countries as far as nuclear proliferation is concerned. We call for the universalization of international instruments in this area.

Kazakhstan has repeatedly put forward proposals to create an international legally binding agreement on the non-use or threat of use of nuclear weapons by nuclear weapon states against non-nuclear-weapon states.

This year, we marked the 10th anniversary of the removal of all nuclear weapons left over by the former Soviet Union on our soil. We are working with our neighbors to establish a nuclear weapons free zone in Central Asia. The treaty establishing the zone is expected to be signed soon at the former Soviet test site at Semipalatinsk, becoming an important milestone in the joint efforts to strengthen the nonproliferation regime.

Making full use of this opportunity, I call on the international community to take meaningful steps to establish effective control over nuclear, chemical and biological materials and their production technologies in order to prevent proliferation of these deadly weapons.

I wish to express my sincere hope this symposium will be instrumental in promoting nonproliferation values throughout the world community.

Once again, I welcome all our distinguished guests and outstanding personalities who have contributed to building a more peaceful and safer world. We appreciate you as reliable partners and sincere friends of Kazakhstan.

Pierre Lellouche
Deputy of the French National Assembly,
President of the NATO Parliamentary Assembly

Pierre Lellouche has been a member of the French National Assembly since 1993 and was recently elected President of the NATO Parliamentary Assembly. He is the Deputy Secretary General of his party, the Union pour un Mouvement Populaire, and a practicing attorney with Clyde and Co., Paris.

From 1989 to 1995, he was Diplomatic Advisor to French President Jacques Chirac, and he has held a number of positions in his party on foreign affairs and defense issues.

Pierre Lellouche was a Co-founder and Deputy Director of the French Institute for International Affairs (IFRI). He has taught and published widely on political-military affairs, including serving as a columnist for le Point and Newsweek.

He is a Vice Chairman of the Atlantic Partnership and a member of the Trilateral Commission and the Council of the International Institute for Strategic Studies. Pierre Lellouche also serves as a Member of the Board of Directors of the Foundation du Futur, and as a member of the editorial board of the European Journal of International Affairs and Journal of Arms Control and Security Studies.

Lellouche is the author of several books including *Le Nouveau Monde* (1992), *La République Immobile* (1998) and *La France et les Bombes* (2000). He was educated in Paris and at Harvard Law School, where he earned his master's and doctorate degrees.

Pierre Lellouche:

"Great" Countries Have Much to Learn From Smaller Ones Who Can Show a Way to Peace

Mr. President, I would like to express my greatest esteem to you on behalf of the French people, French National Assembly, and on the behalf of NATO's Parliamentary Assembly. Kazakhstan is, of course, an associate member of the Assembly, and there is a great cooperation between Kazakhstan and NATO's Partnership for Peace program.

I want to show esteem to you because you reminded us earlier how difficult was the decision you took 15 years ago to shut down nuclear testing and renounce the nuclear arsenal which was the size of France's, UK's and China's combined. Kazakhstan did that. It's not easy. You mentioned your Indian and Pakistani neighbors. One today has to add Iran, and one has to speak of very large nuclear powers in Russia and China.

You took the decision, and that decision is a landmark, I believe, for the world and for humanity.

There is no greater danger today in the world, and I speak here as a Member of Parliament from my capital city Paris, far away from here, but you will soon see the connection, there is no greater danger than the risk of a terrorist group getting a hold of weapons of mass destruction, nuclear weapons.

You have shown, Mr. President, the readiness not only to stop holding nuclear weapons but also to show the way for the rest of the world in which we can convert fissile material that was used in nuclear weapons for civilian use.

In the book you wrote a few years ago, you mentioned your grandmother's bayonet that was turned into a sickle. This morning we saw at the Ulba Plant how very dangerous highly enriched uranium that could be used to produce 20 weapons would now be turned, as a result of the cooperation together between a private organization and the Government of Kazakhstan, into civilian fuel to produce electricity. We have gone from megatons to megawatts. This is an exemplary contribution on the part of Kazakhstan.

I believe, and I say this with much respect, that many 'great' countries have much to learn from smaller countries who are remote but who can show very good examples.

My own country after the Cold War also stopped nuclear testing. We eliminated all land based nuclear missiles, long range and tactical. But, as you said quite lucidly, there is a long way to go. There are much too many weapons still in the hands of the superpowers and in other nuclear powers in general. We need to convince eventual proliferators that we are moving in the right direction.

This is why NTI has been implementing the vision of both my friend Ted Turner and my colleague and friend Senator Nunn. This is why we are working so hard trying to advocate ideas such as the one Mr. Turner just mentioned: lowering the level of alert between the nuclear forces of the great powers. It is unthinkable that 15 years after the end of the Cold War we are still ready to fight a nuclear war in the next five minutes. Something should be done about it.

Secondly, we should get rid of all nuclear materials at research facilities and generalize the example you gave at Ulba, that of transforming highly enriched uranium from research reactors, and there are 150 nuclear reactors in 40 different countries, into civilian fuel.

Lastly, and this is an idea that we discussed with our Russian friends and Director ElBaradei in Moscow this week, to offer the developing world nuclear fuel plants which will provide fuel guaranteed by the IAEA instead of building national enrichment and reprocessing facilities which can be a cause for worry of proliferation.

On all of these issues we need to be working together, and you see here how closely your security is linked to that of other countries.

All of us have the same goal in terms of nuclear security. You have shown an example to the world. And I would like to express our deepest honor to the Kazakh people, esteem and respect to you, Mr. President.

Kenji Murakami
Director of Safeguards
Division of Inspections in the Department of Safeguards
International Atomic Energy Agency

 Kenji Murakami is the Director of Safeguards in the International Atomic Energy Agency's Division of Inspections in the Department of Safeguards. His areas of responsibility include safeguards implementation in all European Union States, Eastern European States, and NIS States (former Soviet Union).

Murakami joined the IAEA in the Department of Safeguards (Operations) in 1982. He was actively involved in inspections as well as negotiations and policy decisions in safeguards with States in North/South America, Africa, North/Eastern Europe and led Iraq Missions in the 1990's.

Since 1992, he has been actively engaged in the technical support and establishment of the nuclear material control systems in the former Soviet Union and the continuing effort to improve the condition of nuclear material accounting and control in the region.

Prior to joining the IAEA, Kenji Murakami had a long experience with nuclear industry, particularly with nuclear reactor and nuclear fuel industry in the USA.

Mohamed ElBaradei:

NTI-Kazakhstan Effort Could Well Serve As Model for Future Projects in Other Countries

Delivered on behalf of Director General Mohamed ElBaradei by Kenji Murakami

The Nuclear Threat Initiative embodies the best features of public-private partnership: a worthy cause; crisply defined, practical objectives; and – in 4 years – a series of concrete achievements, successful steps towards making the world safer and more secure. The vision of former Senator Sam Nunn and CNN founder Ted Turner has proven its value; since its establishment in 2001, NTI has made important contributions towards securing weapon-usable nuclear material and reducing the threat of nuclear terrorism.

The IAEA and its Member States have benefited directly from NTI's assistance and partnership. Shortly after the terrorist attacks of September 2001, when the IAEA was making sweeping revisions to its nuclear security program, NTI pledged $1.15 million to the Agency's Nuclear Security Fund. The Fund has been used to achieve tangible nuclear security improvements: upgrades to physical protection of nuclear facilities and nuclear and radioactive material; urgently needed training in nuclear security for national officials; enhanced detection capabilities at border crossings; and improved national and international readiness for responding to terrorist acts.

NTI has consistently sought to target its contributions to address areas of high priority. A primary point of focus has been to secure (and, where possible, eliminate) material that could be diverted for weapons purposes. In *"Project Vinça"*, NTI committed $5 million in 2002 to help remove high enriched uranium fuel from a research reactor near Belgrade, for return to Russia.

29

The Vinça success led to similar operations in other countries; with support from Russia, the United States and NTI, seven such transfers of fresh fuel back to Russia have been made since 2002 – a total of 112 kilograms of HEU. Current plans foresee further shipments of fresh HEU from another three countries in the next 15 months. The IAEA is also continuing to work on arrangements for the repatriation of spent research reactor fuel of Russian origin.

With this history of activity as a backdrop, the nature of the NTI-Kazakhstan project should come as no surprise. The amount of unused nuclear fuel from the shutdown BN-350 reactor – nearly 3000 kilograms, consisting largely of HEU – made this project a candidate for NTI's interest and involvement. In 2001, Sam Nunn and NTI president Charles Curtis approached the Kazakh Government to offer support for the safe transportation of the fuel to the Ulba Metallurgical Plant JSC (UMP), where it could be dismantled and down-blended into LEU.

Once again, these efforts are bearing fruit. By the end of this year, 2,897 kilograms of HEU – enough to produce dozens of nuclear bombs – will have been down-blended to LEU and placed in safe storage. Throughout the project, the IAEA has been implementing safeguards coverage, with no difficulties experienced. It is noteworthy, in my view, that this project demonstrates the feasibility of developing complex engineering and organizational solutions for converting HEU into commercially valuable material that is not directly usable in nuclear weapons. As such, the NTI-Kazakhstan effort could well serve as a model for future projects in other countries.

As we look at the broader picture of international peace and security, it is clear that much remains to be done. Many aspects of the global security framework are in urgent need of reform. We must press forward with our strategies to protect against nuclear terrorism. We must put in place additional measures to control the spread of sensitive nuclear technology, to guard against proliferation, and to move towards nuclear disarmament. We must continue to work on both the symptoms and root causes of the challenges we face.

But it is equally clear that, on many of these fronts, meaningful progress is achieved one step at a time – through practical, concrete initiatives to fix 'weak links' in the nuclear security. Many countries are making urgent efforts to address these vulnerabilities, and NTI is providing a good example of how civil society can take a leadership role.

I would like to take this opportunity to congratulate the Government of Kazakhstan, as well as the Nuclear Threat Initiative, on this important achievement.

Following the statement of Director ElBaradei,
Kenji Murakami said:
We are thrilled and very honored by yesterday's announcement of the Nobel Peace Prize to the IAEA and Mohamed ElBaradei. It is the highest possible recognition and also public support to our work and to what we have achieved. Our aim in safeguards activity is to be technically correct, impartial and independent in our conclusions. We will continue to work in this vein for the purpose of atomic security.

Vladimir Shkolnik
Minister of Industry and Trade of the Republic of Kazakhstan

 Vladimir Shkolnik has a distinguished career in government and science, and extensive personal involvement in Kazakhstan's nuclear disarmament and the destruction of the Semipalatinsk nuclear test site infrastructure.

Minister Shkolnik serves as Minister of Industry and Trade since January 2006. From January 2002 to January 2006 he served as Minister of Energy and Mineral Resources, and prior to that as Deputy Prime Minister and Minister of Energy and Mineral Resources.

From 1994 to 1999, he served as Minister of Energy, Industry and Trade, Minister of Science and New Technologies, Minister of Science and President of the National Academy of Sciences, and Minister of Science and Higher Education.

Throughout the years since independence, Minister Shkolnik has been closely involved in the disarmament processes in Kazakhstan, including Project Sapphire, which secretly removed 1,278 pounds of highly enriched uranium from Kazakhstan to the U.S. in November 1994.

From 1992 to 1994, Minister Shkolnik served as Director General of Kazakhstan's Atomic Energy Agency, and was personally involved in the early stages of dismantling Kazakhstan's nuclear weapons infrastructure.

For almost twenty years before independence, from 1973 to 1992, Vladimir Shkolnik worked at the Mangyshlak Atomic Energy Combine, also known as BN-350 reactor, where his engineering career started and he rose to the position of Deputy Director for Science, Reactor Manufacturing and Nuclear Safety.

He now serves as President of the Nuclear Society of the Republic of Kazakhstan, and is a member of the Council of the International Science and Technology Center, the International

Council of Scientific Associations, INTAS and other international organizations.

He has written more than 130 scientific publications in areas such as atomic safety engineering, physics of nuclear reactors, mathematical modeling of neutron-physical processes in nuclear power installations, and experimental researches on physical characteristics of nuclear reactors.

Minister Shkolnik holds a degree in nuclear physics from the Moscow Engineering and Physical Institute which he graduated from in 1973. He holds a Doctorate of Science in Physics and Mathematics, and is a Professor. He has been awarded the Order of Parasat.

Vladimir Shkolnik was born in Serpukhov, Russia, in 1949.

Vladimir Shkolnik:

Kazakhstan's Non-Nuclear-Weapons History, The Path from Commitment to Reality

From our first days as an independent country, Kazakhstan has pursued a vision of the future world without nuclear, chemical and other weapons of mass destruction, with continuously shrinking arsenals of conventional armaments. It is a vision of a future where security is guaranteed not by any nuclear or military means, but by political and legal containment through international mechanisms.

In our times, problems of nuclear disarmament and nonproliferation of weapons of mass destruction became intertwined. The achievement of international security is only possible through multilateral efforts of both nuclear and non-nuclear-weapons countries. Preserving and strengthening the regimes of nonproliferation of weapons of mass destruction is one of the most important priorities of Kazakhstan's foreign and domestic policies.

Kazakhstan's first step in this area was shutting down the Semipalatinsk nuclear test site on August 29, 1991. President Nursultan Nazarbayev took this step despite the position of Moscow. At that time, his decision was akin to a decision by the Governor of Nevada to shut down the federal nuclear test site in that state.

Despite all the difficulties of political, social and financial nature connected with the destruction of the weapons, in 1992 Kazakhstan declared it preferred seeking the status of an independent country and membership in the UN as a non-nuclear-weapons state, rather than seeking recognition by the international community as a nuclear power. Since taking that momentous decision, Kazakhstan has steadfastly adhered to our obligations.

Since becoming a legal successor state to the former USSR in connection with the Treaty between the USSR and the USA on the Reduction and Limitation of Strategic Offensive Arms and the Treaty between the USSR and the USA on Eliminating Medium and Short Range Missiles, Kazakhstan has been true to its obligations. Regular inspections of Kazakhstan's facilities under these treaties confirm our full and unwavering observance.

Kazakhstan's accession to the Treaty on Nonproliferation of Nuclear Weapons in 1993 as a non-nuclear-weapons state ended that chapter in Kazakhstan's history which had to do with testing and deployment of nuclear weapons on our territory. Since independence, Kazakhstan has taken a number of specific steps proving our full determination to strengthen the nonproliferation regime and promote global denuclearization using all means possible.

In February 1994, the Republic of Kazakhstan became a member of the International Atomic Energy Agency (IAEA). Currently, all nuclear facilities in Kazakhstan are under full IAEA safeguards. Kazakhstan's firm commitment to international obligations was confirmed by the fact that among the signatories of the Lisbon Protocol Kazakhstan was the first to implement its provisions relating to removing strategic offensive weapons. On April 21, 1995, the process of removing nuclear weapons from Kazakhstan, which took more than a year, was completed. On May 30, 1995, the last nuclear explosive at the Semipalatinsk test site was destroyed. From that moment on, Kazakhstan's soil has been free from nuclear weapons.

Disarmament is both a goal and a means to achieving a safe and nonviolent, stable and prosperous world. It certainly is not the only means. The process of disarmament and control over weapons is one of the directions of international efforts aimed at eliminating the threat of large scale wars. Comprehensive security exists not only because of military security. In equal share, it is also defined by economic wellbeing, social climate, ecological conditions, availability of natural resources and the level of development of communications. Historic experience shows these are the factors which have served as main reasons for tensions in international relations which then grow into military conflicts.

The end of the Cold War led to fundamental changes in the existing security system. The main essence of these changes can be explained by the universalization of values. Countries which ignore basic values such as human rights, economic wellbeing of the society achieved through the rule of law, economic freedom and social justice can be described as isolated islands. This means that today, as never before, principal decisions are possible which can ensure a safe and secure future for mankind. As a fully fledged member of the international community, Kazakhstan spares no efforts in adopting and implementing these values.

On May 11, 1995, important decisions were made at the NPT Treaty Review Conference in New York relating to the treaty's permanent prolongation, raising the effectiveness of the treaty, the principles and the role of nuclear nonproliferation and disarmament, as well as to the creation of an improved mechanism to control execution of the treaty's provisions. Having voted for the NPT extension, countries voted for their national independence. The path towards such decisions was bumpy, often dramatic. Reason prevailed, however, reflecting the realities of modern days and imperatives of the immediate future. In addition to South Africa, which promoted extension through the strength of the authority it commanded, Kazakhstan's position also carried special weight since it came from a country which, for the first time in history, had renounced nuclear weapons it once possessed.

Nuclear disarmament is impossible without control over the production of fissile material. That is why Kazakhstan considers it a priority to develop an agreement prohibiting the production of highly enriched uranium and plutonium for the production of nuclear weapons. The first step in this direction should be the start of negotiations on signing an agreement prohibiting production of fissile material with the participation of all producing states. The next step should be the elimination of all stockpiles of such materials under strict supervision of the

International Atomic Energy Agency. Examples to follow can be found in blending down 200 tons of highly enriched uranium at U.S. facilities to be used as fuel for nuclear power plants and the transfer to the United States of approximately 600 kilograms of highly enriched uranium by Kazakhstan under IAEA control. One needs to take into account that with approximately 25 percent of the world's natural uranium ore reserves, Kazakhstan used to supply 33 percent of uranium production and 85 percent of nuclear fuel for atomic facilities in the former USSR.

Given the need for comprehensive strengthening of the non-proliferation regime and creation of favorable conditions for actually eliminating nuclear weapons, Kazakhstan had promoted the speediest conclusion of negotiations on a full and comprehensive ban on nuclear tests, calling this issue the priority for participants of the Disarmament Conference as early as 1995.

The initiative of the countries of Central Asia, expressed in the Almaty Declaration of February 28, 1997, to establish a nuclear weapons free zone in the region was another step toward strengthening the nonproliferation regime. In terms of its political significance, we can compare it to events such as the accession of Central Asian countries to the Treaty on Nonproliferation of Nuclear Weapons and the removal of nuclear weapons from Kazakhstan's territory.

Coupled with principled and consistent position on the permanent prolongation of the NPT Treaty as the symbol of international peace and full elimination of nuclear weapons, Kazakhstan believes there must be a treaty on full and comprehensive nuclear disarmament.

The proliferation of weapons of mass destruction, nuclear, chemical, and biological, and their means of delivery and dual use technologies presents significant threat at regional and global levels.

Speaking of the region of Central Asia, we need to take into account the existing situation. Nuclear ambitions of certain Asian countries and the existence of local military conflicts create the opportunity for international terrorists to acquire and use weapons of mass destruction. At the same time, the existing level of social and economic development for many Asian countries creates major difficulties in ensuring reliable customs and export controls. Research and development work in some countries of the region in areas of technology of production for weapons of mass destruction and their means of delivery, including intercontinental ballistic missiles are also of serious concern.

The state introduces controls over external trade in nuclear materials, equipment and technologies of dual use as a component of WMD nonproliferation policies. This has to do with the fact that the main danger lies in terrorist groups or countries supporting them acquiring materials, equipment and technologies used in WMD production.

The Law on Export Control of Kazakhstan of June 18, 1996, the first such law adopted in the countries of the Commonwealth of Independent States, has established principles and rules of export control over weapons, military equipment, raw materials, products, technologies of special application, scientific and technological information. This law thus ensured the interests of both international and national security. The law determined the main principles for export control, the key parts of which are observing the international obligations in nonproliferation of weapons of mass destruction and other types of weapons, priority of political interests in ensuring export controls, as well as full governmental control over exports of nuclear materials and technologies.

Therefore, the important result of Kazakhstan's nuclear policies is the fact that the republic, having unequivocally determined its position for nonproliferation of WMD, has brought major contributions to nuclear disarmament. Positive reaction of the international community towards Kazakhstan's actions manifests itself in international assistance which nuclear states provide to Kazakhstan, primarily in the area of eliminating nuclear weapons infrastructure.

Cooperative Threat Reduction Program

The Cooperative Threat Reduction (CTR) program took root in the fall of 1991. At the end of September of that year, U.S. President George H.W. Bush offered to discuss with the Soviet Union the possibility of cooperation in ensuring secure and environmentally safe measures for storage, transportation and dismantling of nuclear weapons, as well as measures to improve physical protection for them.

The Act on Soviet Military Threat Reduction, signed into law on December 12, 1991, provided US$400 million in financing for these goals. Later, in October 1993, that act was expanded by a new Act on Cooperative Threat Reduction.

The new law provided details of the assistance program and included projects to eliminate other types of weapons of mass destruction which are regulated were bilateral agreements between the USA and the countries of the former Soviet Union.

The CTR program joins efforts to reduce the military threat and is one of the key instruments of preventing this threat. It is primarily aimed at the reduction in current and future threats to security of the United States.

The goals of Kazakhstan and the United States in nonproliferation and the reduction of nuclear risks are the same. This was one of the key reasons for Kazakhstan's active involvement in joint projects under the program. In December 1993, Kazakhstan and the United States signed a Framework Agreement on elimination of silos for intercontinental ballistic missiles, elimination of consequences of emergency situations and prevention of proliferation of nuclear weapons. At the same time, five executive agreements were also signed calling for practical implementation of specific directions of cooperation. During the years from 1995 to 2000, more details for programs were elaborated and acted upon, and the cooperation continually expanded.

The Framework Agreement had a term of seven years with an option for extension. In December 2000, the two countries extended the Agreement for another seven years, until the end of 2007. Currently, close to a dozen CTR executive agreements between the United States and Kazakhstan are active. The 1993 Framework Agreement and the executive agreements determine the character of CTR programs in Kazakhstan.

The CTR program in Kazakhstan is aimed at ensuring the country meets its obligations under the START-1 Treaty, at the environmentally safe elimination of infrastructure of nuclear and other weapons of mass destruction, prevention of the proliferation of WMD, military cooperation and conversion of military technologies to civilian use, creation of an effective system of export controls, safe elimination of nuclear materials and the expansion of scientific and technical cooperation.

During the sealing of the last test tunnel at the Semipalatinsk test site on July 29, 2000, an amendment to the Framework Agreement was signed adding a new dimension to the joint activities: prevention of proliferation of materials and technologies of dual use.

One can note an interesting pattern in the development of CTR. As the projects are implemented and as the two countries do more joint work, they expand the scope of cooperation and find new avenues for it. While the CTR program started with the elimination of strategic offensive arms and nuclear weapons infrastructure, contacts between defense departments and customs services have intensified. The spectrum of exchanges of scientific and technical information coupled with technologies capable of being used in civilian activities was also expanded. The program expanded to include safe burial of spent nuclear fuel from the BN-350 reactor and safe decommissioning of the reactor itself.

The basis for conducting work on CTR projects in this area was created with the signing of an executive agreement "On long-term storage of nuclear materials from BN-350" between the U.S. Department of Energy and Kazakhstan's Ministry of Energy and Mineral Resources on November 17, 1997. This agreement provided for long term storage of spent fuel at the BN-350 site.

Significance of the project on down-blending of highly enriched uranium

A new project, "Safe transportation and down-blending of highly enriched uranium contained in fresh BN-350 reactor fuel", started in 2002. Senator Sam Nunn and Charles Curtis, President of the Nuclear Threat Initiative (NTI) initiated the project, offering the Government of Kazakhstan assistance with it.

The project was implemented in coordination with, and under the control of, the IAEA.

Among the objectives of the program to safely remove nuclear materials from the territory of the Mangyshlak Atomic Energy Combine (MAEC) was the transportation of fresh fuel from its BN-350 reactor, stockpiled, but never used during the operation of the reactor. Highly enriched reactor fuel is a dual use material. Its second application is as ready-made material for nuclear bombs. Approximately 2,900 kilograms of nuclear fuel, part of which was highly enriched uranium, had to be put risk-free conditions preventing its illegal use forever.

The NTI-Kazatomprom Project included two components: transportation of highly enriched uranium from MAEC and its down-blending to low enriched uranium. After down-blending, this material can no longer be used in weapons production while it preserves its usefulness for civilian purposes.

The project's main objective was to 'strengthen global security through reducing the risk of use of weapons of mass destruction.' The project's main result is the down-blending of 2,900 kilograms of fresh fuel meant for the BN-350 reactor (classified at the start of the project as nuclear material of dual use) into low enriched nuclear material. Currently, the material is in safe storage and remains under IAEA safeguards and creates no threat of nonproliferation.

The project confirmed the reality and practicality of complex design and organizational solutions in such sensitive area as processing nuclear materials. Most certainly, it became yet

41

another indicator of the huge benefits of mutual cooperation for peace and security.

Kazakhstan boldly adopts this approach because our country stands for strengthening international security, developing cooperation among all countries and enlarging the role of international organizations in finding solutions for global problems and conflicts.

Susan Eisenhower
President Emeritus and Senior Fellow
The Eisenhower Institute

 Susan Eisenhower is President of the Eisenhower Group, Inc, which provides strategic counsel on political, business and public affairs projects. Ms. Eisenhower has consulted for major companies doing business overseas such as IBM, American Express, Diebold Corporation and Loral Space Systems and she is a Senior Director of Stonebridge International, a Washington-based international consulting firm chaired by former National Security Advisor, Samuel "Sandy" Berger.

At the same time, she is the President Emeritus and a Distinguished Fellow of the Eisenhower Institute, where she served as both president and chairman. After more than twenty years in the foreign affairs field she is best known for her work in Russia and the former Soviet Union. During that time, Ms. Eisenhower has testified before the Senate Armed Services and Senate Budget Committees on policy toward that region. She has also been appointed to the National Academy of Sciences' standing Committee on International Security and Arms Control (CISAC) where she is now serving a fourth term. In 2000, a year before September 11, she co-edited a book, *Islam and Central Asia*, which carried the prescient subtitle, *An Enduring Legacy or an Evolving Threat?*

Ms. Eisenhower has served on many government task forces. In the spring of 2000, the Secretary of Energy appointed Ms. Eisenhower to a blue ribbon task force, the Baker-Cutler Commission, to evaluate U.S. funded nuclear nonproliferation programs in Russia, and since that time she has served as an advisor on another DOE study. In the fall of 2001, after serving two terms on the NASA Advisory Council she was appointed to serve on the International Space Station Management and Cost Evaluation Task Force, which analyzed ISS management and cost overruns. She is currently a member of the Secretary of Energy's Task Force on Nuclear Energy. She has also served as an Academic Fellow of the International Peace and Security program of Carnegie Corporation of New York, and is a director of the Carnegie Endowment for International Peace and the Nuclear Threat Initiative, co-chaired by Senator Sam Nunn and Ted Turner.

Susan Eisenhower has spoken at many diverse types of gatherings: from Harvard and UCLA; World Affairs Councils; and corporate gatherings; to specialist audiences, such as the one assembled at the Army War College, where she gave the 1998 Commandant's Lecture. She has also given full speeches, by invitation, at other prominent places, such as: the National Press Club, the Smithsonian Institution, the National Archives, the Hollywood Bowl, The French National Assembly, and the White House.

Ms. Eisenhower's first professional experience was as a writer. In the 1970s Ms. Eisenhower lived overseas for six years, first while a student at the American University in Paris and then as a London resident and stringer for *The Saturday Evening Post*. Later she wrote a column for Wolfe Newspapers and went on to write for business. Within the last ten years, Ms. Eisenhower has authored three books: two of which, Breaking Free and Mrs. Ike, have appeared on regional best seller lists. She has also edited four collected volumes on regional security issues – the most recent, *Partners in Space* (2004) – and penned hundreds of op-eds and articles on foreign policy for publications such as *The Washington Post, The Los Angeles Times, USA Today, the Naval Institute's Proceedings, The London Spectator,* and *Gannett Newspapers.* She has provided analysis for CNN International, MSNBC, Nightline, World News Tonight with Peter Jennings, This Week with David Brinkley, CBS Sunday Morning, Good Morning America, The News Hour with Jim Lehrer, Fox News and Hardball, as well as NPR and other nation-wide television and radio programs.

Susan Eisenhower:

Man's Miraculous Inventiveness Should Not Be Dedicated to Death, But Consecrated to Life... That Is What Kazakhstan Has Done

It is a pleasure and an honor for me to be here today. My husband, Roald Sagdeev regrets that he is not able to be with us. He, too, knows Kazakhstan well and, as a scientist, has also worked on nuclear issues.

Over the years, I have had the opportunity to visit Russian nuclear weapons facilities as part of the U.S. Department of Energy task force, the Baker-Cutler Commission, on U.S.-funded nonproliferation programs in Russia. And, just last week I visited the Nevada test site and went on to Yucca Mountain, which will be the federal depository of spent nuclear fuel in the United States.

Today we had the opportunity to the visit the Ulba nuclear facility and to see the important work that has been undertaken in cooperation with the Nuclear Threat Initiative to blend down highly enriched uranium. All are important aspects of the nuclear question that we are dealing with.

In my travels around the world, it has been extraordinary to see the way that this country, Kazakhstan, and others in the Soviet Union, have handled that Cold War legacy. Those in my age group and older remember well the Cold War and the psychological terror that these weapons imposed on populations across the world. Imagine, today 10,000 Soviet era nuclear warheads have been blended down into commercially usable fuel, which currently electrifies many of America's cities. This is indeed an extraordinary achievement.

I would also like to add my voice to the others in congratulating the IAEA and to Mohammed ElBaradei for winning the Nobel Peace Prize. The IAEA was, of course, established as an outgrowth of United States' peace proposal that was announced at the United Nations in 1953 by my grandfather, Dwight

Eisenhower. It was at that time that he said that the United States is fully committed, as the world should be, to solving the atomic dilemma, and that man's miraculous inventiveness should not be dedicated to his death, but consecrated to his life.

In fact, that is what Kazakhstan has done and in the process has shown the road to peace, and pointed the way to development. In that context I would offer my respect and homage to your President, Nursultan Nazarbayev. It has been his leadership and, indeed, his statesmanship that has made the difference in showing the non-nuclear way forward for other countries, especially in this complex international environment.

I would like to quote from President Nazarbayev's book, *Epicenter of Peace*. I personally found it a very moving story, and if may also say, quite poetic in many ways. He says at the end of one very strong and powerful chapter: "At the end of the twentieth century we have put down our nuclear weapons, voluntarily and ahead of schedule, and we have shown the world what the twenty first century must be."

Kanat Saudabayev
Ambassador Extraordinary and Plenipotentiary of the
Republic of Kazakhstan to the United States of America

 Ambassador Saudabayev, assigned to Washington since December 2000, brings an important contribution strengthening the growing strategic partnership between Kazakhstan and the United States of America in the spheres of security, economy and democratic development.

Before his appointment to the U.S., Ambassador Saudabayev had a long career in the fields of government, diplomacy and the arts.

In 1999 and 2000, he served as the head of the Prime Minister's Office with the rank of Cabinet member. In the 1990s, he served as Kazakhstan's Ambassador to the United Kingdom of Great Britain and Northern Ireland, and was the first Ambassador to Turkey. During 1994, as the Minister of Foreign Affairs, Ambassador Saudabayev worked to implement the developing foreign policy of his young independent state. He was Kazakhstan's signatory to NATO's Partnership for Peace agreement.

In the fall of 1991, he became the last Soviet Ambassador ever appointed, to Turkey, by President Mikhail S. Gorbachev. As he was planning to take up his post, the Soviet Union ceased to exist. Within weeks he was on his way to Turkey again, but as the first Ambassador ever from an independent Kazakhstan.

Working in Moscow from September 1991 through May 1992 as the Plenipotentiary Representative of the Kazakh Soviet Socialist Republic to the USSR, and then, after the Soviet Union collapsed, to the new Russian republic, Kanat Saudabayev was a direct participant in and a witness to many crucial events of those historic days.

Before entering the diplomatic service, Ambassador Saudabayev had a distinguished cultural career, serving as Chairman of the State Committee of Culture with the rank of

Minister, Chairman of the State Film Committee, and Deputy Culture Minister. He began his career as a theatrical producer.

Ambassador Saudabayev holds degrees from the Leningrad Institute of Culture and the Academy of Public Sciences of the Central Committee of Communist Party of the Soviet Union. He has a Ph.D. in Philosophy from the Kazakh State University and a Ph.D. in Political Science from the Moscow State University. His service has been recognized by the Orders of Otan (Fatherland), the highest award in Kazakhstan, and Kurmet (Distinguished Service).

Kanat Saudabayev was born in the Almaty region in 1946.

Since Independence, Kazakhstan's History
Confirms Our Choice Was the Only Right One

A poet once wrote, "When face to face, one cannot see the face: the big thing can only be seen from afar."

Today, we have the opportunity to really see the big thing with our own eyes: the successful completion in Kazakhstan of a unique project in nonproliferation, another powerful demonstration of Kazakhstan's very real contribution to world security and nuclear disarmament.

Fifty-six years ago testing of nuclear weapons began on our ancient land, bringing incalculable suffering to our people. Today, on this land of what is now an independent, democratic and dynamically developing Kazakhstan, we have gathered together to see how the atom can be directed to creation, not destruction, through the efforts of people of good will. The path Kazakhstan has taken in partnership with the international community can be a model for other countries and shows the way forward to a safer world. That was exactly the praise for Kazakhstan the United States Senate offered in a recent unanimously adopted resolution on the occasion of the tenth anniversary of the withdrawal of all nuclear weapons from Kazakhstan.

People often say history does not have a 'what if' clause. Still, we can imagine what could have been if not for the decisiveness and vision of remarkable people in different corners of the world who are with us today, in person and in spirit.

When Kazakhstan stood at the threshold of our independence 14 years ago, the most complex decision President Nursultan Nazarbayev faced was about the future of nuclear weapons in Kazakhstan, which, as we know, constituted the world's fourth largest nuclear arsenal. When the Soviet Union collapsed, nuclear weapons were left in Russia, Belarus, Ukraine and in Kazakhstan. While Russia became the legal successor to

49

the USSR, and while there were no major doubts about which way Belarus and Ukraine would go with their nuclear weapons since they were European countries with mostly Slavic and Christian populations, the situation with Kazakhstan was different.

Situated in Asia and with a sizeable Muslim population, our country faced much greater temptation and had to deal with very eloquent tempters. Kazakhstan's first days of independence saw no lack of emissaries of all sorts who urged our President to keep nuclear weapons, saying: "You will be the first and only Muslim state with nuclear weapons. You will be respected, and the entire world will have to reckon with you." I was witness to such visits and heard arguments of these tempters about Boeing airplanes full of dollars. I have to say a significant part of Kazakhstan's elite at that time was also in favor of keeping our nuclear potential. That is why today it would be fair to say that it was President Nursultan Nazarbayev who made the courageous and historic choice to renounce the nuclear weapons.

Fourteen years ago the Soviet Union was in its death throes, and two men in the United Stated had the clearest understanding of the problems arising from the impending collapse of a nuclear power with tens of thousands of nuclear warheads. It was these two men, Senators Sam Nunn and Richard Lugar, who were able to initiate and get through Congress, despite mistrust and rejection, a bill introducing a revolutionary principle. It called for the U.S. to voluntarily undertake to provide money for the elimination and security of nuclear weapons of its former Cold War adversary. This was unheard of, this was unbelievable, but this was the demonstration of true vision and leadership of these two men. Today our country and the entire world are grateful to them for the Cooperative Threat Reduction Production, better known as the Nunn-Lugar Program.

The whole history of Kazakhstan's further development and our cooperation with the USA in ridding our country of the hideous nuclear legacy confirms our choice was the only right one.

The unprecedented down-blending project which we celebrate today and which brought major contribution to global security in these tense times is the best new evidence Kazakhstan's decision was right. This project has shown Kazakhstan has a yet untapped potential for cooperation in nonproliferation and a huge scientific and technical and human potential for peaceful development of nuclear energy. Finally, this project shows the highest level of confidence between Kazakhstan and the United States and the determination of our governments and responsible citizens of our nations to strengthen our cooperation in the future.

The history of nuclear disarmament in Kazakhstan is a history of selfless and tireless work and sacrifice of thousands of people in Kazakhstan, the United States and many other countries. There are many of these people in this hall today who have answered the call of duty and the call of heart and are committed to the ideals of nonproliferation, doing everything possible to protect the mankind from the danger of weapons of mass destruction. Yet, I am completely convinced that had it not been for the wisdom, courage and vision of President Nazarbayev, Senator Nunn and Senator Lugar, the nuclear history of Kazakhstan and the entire world would have been very different. Their names are already inscribed in golden letters in the history of Kazakhstan, and I am deeply convinced the world will still come around and fully appreciate their outstanding and noble actions.

Today, the threat of proliferation of weapons of mass destruction and the aspirations of international terrorists to acquire and use such weapons have become the most dangerous threats to our planet. That is why I am convinced that we not only can but must talk about Kazakhstan's history of disarmament in cooperation with the international community and about our responsible approach to world security as real and better alternatives to nuclear weapons as means to strengthen authority and further national interests. A meaningful discussion of this subject took place at a symposium at the U.S. Senate in December 2003, which we jointly arranged with Senator

Nunn, and I view today's event as an important advance of this movement.

There are very few people in the world, apart from those leaders who are here with us today, who have greater moral authority to call for active cooperation of all countries in nonproliferation and whose opinion about Kazakhstan's contribution and ways to solve complex problems in this area could carry more weight. They are the soul and the driving force of the nonproliferation movement. I am confident that their opinion and their calls will be heard and that through joint efforts we will be able to build a safer world.

Sam Nunn
Co-chairman and Chief Executive Officer, Nuclear Threat Initiative, Former United States Senator (D-GA)

Sam Nunn is Co-chairman and Chief Executive Officer of the Nuclear Threat Initiative. He served as a U.S. Senator from Georgia for 24 years (1972-1996) and is retired from the law firm of King & Spalding.

Senator Nunn attended Georgia Tech, Emory University and Emory Law School, where he graduated with honors in 1962. After active duty service in the U.S. Coast Guard, he served six years in the U.S. Coast Guard Reserve. He first entered politics as a Member of the Georgia House of Representatives in 1968.

During his tenure in the U.S. Senate, Senator Nunn served as Chairman of the Senate Armed Services Committee and the Permanent Subcommittee on Investigations. He also served on the Intelligence and Small Business Committees. His legislative achievements include the landmark Department of Defense Reorganization Act, drafted with the late Senator Barry Goldwater, and the Nunn-Lugar Cooperative Threat Reduction Program, which provides assistance to Russia and the former Soviet republics for securing and destroying their excess nuclear, biological and chemical weapons.

In addition to his work with NTI, Senator Nunn has continued his service in the public policy arena as a Distinguished Professor in the Sam Nunn School of International Affairs at Georgia Tech and as Chairman of the Board of the Center for Strategic and International Studies in Washington, D.C.

Sam Nunn:

Kazakhstan's Actions, Continued Leadership and Tremendous Job in Nonproliferation Stand as Models for the 21st Century

President Nazarbayev, it is wonderful to be with you again and to be in Kazakhstan again, and particularly in Eastern Kazakhstan and to have the chance to tour the Ulba Metallurgical Plant this morning. I want to acknowledge all the officials of Kazakhstan here today and also the ambassadors from other countries. Thank you very much to the people and the leaders of Kazakhstan for their kind welcome of the Nuclear Threat Initiative, and for being such an outstanding partner in our common efforts to reduce the threat of weapons of mass destruction.

We're delighted to celebrate today the success of a very important joint project between NTI and Kazakhstan.

Kazakhstan's leadership in nonproliferation began with its 1994 decision to give up nuclear weapons. At that time, Kazakhstan had more than 1,400 nuclear weapons – more than France, Britain and China combined. And I remember how important that was. At that time, Senator Lugar and I came to Kazakhstan and met with your President. He told us he was going to give up nuclear weapons and I know what a powerful influence it was in the overall decision of Ukraine, Belarus, and Kazakhstan to get rid of nuclear weapons.

But Kazakhstan's role and President Nazarbayev's role did not end there. Kazakhstan proved itself a leader again with Project Sapphire, a joint project with the United States to secure, and then blend down, 600 kilograms of weapons grade uranium. Today, as we face the threat of more nations – and also perhaps most importantly terrorist groups – acquiring nuclear weapons, Kazakhstan's actions, the continued leadership and the tremendous job in this area stand as models for the kind of leadership and cooperation that is essential in the 21st century.

Today, the most potentially devastating threat is a terrorist attack with nuclear weapons. The most effective and least expensive way to prevent nuclear terrorism is to keep nuclear materials out of the hands of terrorists. The project we are celebrating today advances those aims and sets an example for the direction of the world.

Today, we mark the success of the joint NTI-Kazatomprom project to permanently remove and eliminate nuclear fuel containing 2,897 kilograms of highly enriched uranium from the BN-350 fast breeder power reactor in Aktau – turning it into safe, non-weapons usable forms of uranium for use in commercial and in scientific activities.

To each of the leaders of this project that are here with us today, and to each of the dedicated men and women who work every day at the Ulba Plant and to our own NTI staff, to Laura Holgate and Bob Schultz in particular, on behalf of the Board of NTI, and I believe on behalf of the people of the world, I say 'thank you, thank you, thank you, you've all done a magnificent job'.

This project began with discussions in 2001 and 2002. It involved moving highly enriched uranium fuel by rail safely across the country to the Ulba Metallurgical Plant, where it was then in large part blended down. Costs were shared equally from the beginning between NTI and Kazatomprom, and material that could have made as many as two dozen bombs was eliminated.

This project has in a very concrete and measurable way reduced the opportunity for terrorists to acquire nuclear weapons, and as Director General ElBaradei said, we hope it will serve as a model for future projects in other countries. I want to thank Director ElBaradei for that wonderful message he sent. I also want to say that not only was the Nobel Peace award very well deserved by Director ElBaradei and IAEA but most importantly, I hope it will get countries around the globe give more authority, more support and more resources to the IAEA in their continuing important mission.

The project we are celebrating today is especially important for the following reasons. It is not just that we are making the highly enriched uranium more secure at the reactor site and thus harder to steal – we are eliminating it as a fuel at this site, and thus making it impossible to steal.

NTI is very proud of our partnership with Kazakhstan. The threat of nuclear terrorism puts us in a race between cooperation and catastrophe. The kind of cooperation we see again and again from Kazakhstan on a continuing basis can help us win that race. While many other nations are walking or crawling, Kazakhstan is running, and we thank you, Mr. President, and we thank the people of Kazakhstan.

President Nazarbayev: on behalf of NTI and all who are made more secure by your leadership, and I think that includes the entire world, I would like to present you with this sign of our gratitude. It's a crystal pyramid entitled "Vision" – in honor of your ability to look to the future and see a better path to peace. Thank you, Mr. President, for seeing opportunities that others don't – and for acting on those opportunities. You have shown and you are showing us the way to a safer world.

2002-2006 Highly Enriched Uranium Down-Blending Project: The Makings of the Success

By Ruslan Ibraev, Viktor Kossenko, Olga Tyupkina, and Robert Schultz

I. Introduction
Nonproliferation as a factor in strengthening the global security system

A reliable global security system is key to the stability of the modern world. However, its operational effectiveness is affected by many different factors. One of these is the ever-higher accomplishments in science and technology. It has become increasingly clear that, although the progress in science and technology can have a very positive impact upon our lives, it is a double-edged sword. The advances in science, declining costs of production and improved access to technology, which promise so many benefits for human civilization, can also be perverted by criminals and terrorists.

In response, the global security system has to be as flexible and rapidly changing as progress itself in order to identify and control the potential negative applications of new knowledge and technologies. This is a complex and difficult task. Historically, the world has relied upon the most advanced nations to provide this 'service', but the spread of technology challenges this approach because it potentially enables not just smaller countries but also criminal organizations to threaten civilized societies as terrorist attacks in the last few years have demonstrated.

Nonproliferation is an essential component of the necessary response to this threat. Strict control over weapons of mass destruction, the materials used to make them, and dual use technologies must be the primary functions of the global security system, and are essential to containing terrorism and thwarting the military aspirations of rogue countries.

CTR Experience in Kazakhstan

The Cooperative Threat Reduction (CTR) program was established by the U.S. to reduce the existing and future threats to global security, and has become a model for international collaboration in the security arena. Each new CTR project has also helped develop the CTR program itself, widening the scope of activities, increasing the complexity of the goals and tasks, and increasing the number of participants. The CTR projects in Kazakhstan demonstrate all of those aspects very well.

The last decade has been particularly difficult for Kazakhstan. In 1992, Kazakhstan became the fourth largest nuclear power in the world at a time of considerable political instability and economic difficulty. Public opinion in Kazakhstan on this matter was divided, with one part wishing to retain nuclear weapons and the other seeking a nonproliferation approach. Although the Kazakhstan's press and public opinion were not fully supportive of his action, President Nursultan Nazarbayev declared Kazakhstan a non-nuclear-weapons country. This act defined the future strategy of Kazakhstan in the sphere of global security, and nonproliferation became a core element in its foreign and domestic political strategies.

Thus, the USA and Kazakhstan had similar goals with respect to nonproliferation and reduction of the threat presented by weapons of mass destruction. The intent to support nonproliferation was the main reason for Kazakhstan joining the CTR program.

Kazakhstan had gained a great deal of experience in the implementation of CTR Projects by 2001. This began in 1993 with the elimination of strategic weapons and much of the nuclear weapons infrastructure which existed at that time in Kazakhstan. In 1995, the CTR priority shifted to the elimination of the infrastructure at the former Semipalatinsk Test Site

(STS) which had supported the nuclear weapons program and, in 1996, this part of the program was expanded to include the elimination of biological weapons infrastructure at Stepnogorsk. By 1999, the CTR Program had been expanded again to include a particular focused on strengthening protection systems for biological weapons materials.

In the fall of 2000, the CTR program in Kazakhstan reached a major milestone. The five-year program to eliminate the nuclear weapon infrastructure at STS was completed, and documents setting out new directions for the CTR program were signed. These new directions focused on preventing the proliferation of dual use materials and technologies, and allowed work to start on the safe disposition of BN-350 reactor fuel and decommissioning of the BN-350 fast breeder reactor.

The BN-350 reactor was one of four energy facilities at the Mangyshlak Atomic Energy Complex (MAEC), located close to the city of Aktau in the western Kazakhstan. The MAEC site is located in the coastal zone approximately four kilometers from the Caspian Sea and provides the adjacent regions with electricity and drinking water produced by desalination of seawater.

The BN-350 reactor was shut down for decommissioning in 1999 after almost 26 years of operation. Decommissioning the reactor is a complex task which will require significant investments and the development of unique engineering solutions. It is projected to take at least 10 years with a total investment of more than $100 million for dismantling the reactor and the safe storage of nuclear materials and radioactive waste.

At the time the reactor was closed, some 300 metric tons of spent BN-350 fuel were stored at the reactor site, containing three metric tons of weapons grade plutonium. The U.S. Department of Energy has spent more than $61 million between 1997 and 2004 on material protection control and accounting (MPC&A) for the spent fuel, and on the irreversible shutdown and decommissioning of the reactor itself. This work included safeguarding the fuel to meet IAEA standards, and packaging it into 2,800 containers manufactured in Kazakhstan to DOE specifications. Current work addresses the long-term storage of the fuel and its potential transportation to a spent fuel disposal facility.

In addition to the U.S., other states have also contributed to this program, including the United Kingdom and France through the European Union's TACIS program, as well as Japan.

II. Nuclear Threat Initiative (NTI) Kazakhstan's Project
Safe transportation and down-blending of highly enriched uranium contained in fresh BN-350 reactor fuel

One of the tasks of the program on safe disposal of nuclear materials from the MAEC site became the elimination of highly enriched uranium (HEU) contained in the unused BN-350 reactor fuel which remained at the MAEC site following the final shutdown of the reactor. This HEU is potentially usable as a raw material for nuclear bombs. About 2,900 kg of nuclear fuel, a large part of which was highly enriched uranium, was stored at MAEC. In 2001, Senator Sam Nunn, and NTI president, Charles B. Curtis, approached the Kazakhstan's Government to offer support in the safe transportation of the fuel to the Ulba Metallurgical Plant (UMP), where it could be dismantled and down-blended into low enriched uranium that cannot be used for weapon production.

The NTI project in Kazakhstan began in 2002, and consisted of four phases:

1. Development of the technical scope of the project and the expert review and official coordination of the working plans and technical tasks.
2. Obtaining necessary licenses and authorizations, and the transportation of the BN-350 fuel from the MAEC site to the UMP site.
3. Upgrading physical protection system at UMP as appropriate for storage and processing of Category 1 nuclear materials.

4. Dismantling of the BN-350 fuel and down-blending of the HEU to LEU.

These phases are described in more detail below.

The principal executors of the project were:

NTI (Nuclear Threat Initiative), a U.S. not-for-profit charitable organization, was formed in January 2001. NTI's mission is to strengthen global security by reducing the risk of proliferation of nuclear, biological and chemical weapons. NTI aims to attract public support for nonproliferation activities, to promote the development of new thinking, and to support the reduction of the threat presented by weapons of mass destruction. NTI provided funds to support the project in accordance with these goals.

Kazatomprom CJSC, a state owned commercial organization linking leading enterprises of Kazakhstan's uranium industry, is responsible for the import and export of uranium and other industrial materials. Kazatomprom was founded in July 1997 and as the owner of the UMP, is responsible to the Government of Kazakhstan for ensuring all nuclear safety requirements are met during the project.

Ulba Metallurgical Plant JSC is the company which performed the uranium processing and nuclear fuel production. The company is widely recognized for its high quality nuclear fuel production capability, and for safe and reliable operations with nuclear fuel which have international certification according to the ISO 9002 quality standard. In addition to its uranium operations, UMP produces high quality products of beryllium, tantalum, and niobium. UMP was responsible for planning all legal, technical and operational aspects of the project, and for its execution.

Nonproliferation Support Center (NSC), a Kazakhstan not-for-profit nongovernmental organization founded in December 2002 on the basis of the former Institute of Nonproliferation. NSC is an association of organizations occupied with scientific and technical activity in the field of nonproliferation. NSC was responsible for managing the work on the first stage of the NTI Project, developing of all working plans including the transportation of the BN-350 fuel to UMP and the subsequent storage and down-blending of the HEU.

III. Phase One:
Development of plans for the safe transportation and down-blending of HEU contained in the BN-350 reactor fuel

The first phase of the project took place between February and August 2002, and included the development and expert review of plans in the following areas: obtaining authorizations and licenses; identifying the most suitable transportation route; selecting the technology to be used for the down-blending process and installation of down-blending facilities; environmental impact analysis; quality control; safety management; project management and coordination; and personnel training. Kazakhstan's nuclear materials and safety experts, under the supervision of the Ministry of Energy and Mineral Resources of the Republic of Kazakhstan, prepared relevant documents.

The planning work included a review of the logistics and security aspects of the available transportation modes, rail, road and air. It was decided to transport the BN-350 fuel from MAEC to UMP by rail, with accompanying armed guards, as this provided the greatest level of security.

Planning for the work at UMP covered the installation of new facilities as required to store and down-blend the highly enriched uranium, including the dismantling of old equipment and the purchase and/or fabrication of new equipment, as well as putting in place amendments to the operating licenses held by UMP to allow storage and processing of HEU.

During the planning phase, the need for improved physical protection systems at UMP to cover the storage and down-blending of the HEU was identified, and a separate work phase to address these improvements was added to the project.

An analysis of Kazakhstan's national legislation, together with instructions and directions from the IAEA and national agencies regulating nuclear operations in Kazakhstan, was completed to assist with execution of the program.

Secure handling of nuclear materials requires the maintenance of strict confidentiality regarding the schedule and places of work, and the systems for physical protection of the materials. Consequently, information was made available on a "need to know" basis only to those people with appropriate authorizations and clearances, and only as required for them to discharge their responsibilities. Coordination of the large number of experts, each of whom was involved in only part of the project, was a significant management task.

The project planning was complex and required integration of activities of a large number of agencies and enterprises involved in the project, as well as identifying appropriate experts for each of the project elements. The plans set out in Phase 1 proved to have been successfully developed, with only minor adjustments needed during the course of the project.

IV. Phase Two:
Approval of work plans, transportation of the BN-350 fuel and licensing of the facilities for its subsequent storage and down-blending

The second phase of the project ran from June 2002 to September 2003. Its main tasks were ratification of the plans developed during the first phase of the project, transportation of the BN-350 fuel to UMP, and obtaining the licenses for the storage and downblending facilities at UMP.

Ratification of the Plans. Documents prepared in Phase I were subjected to two levels of expert review-by independent experts and by supervisory bodies of the Republic of Kazakhstan. The Atomic Energy Committee of the Republic of Kazakhstan (KAEC) ensured that they complied with the official requirements of the Republic of Kazakhstan and with international requirements and norms for handling Category 1 nuclear materials. Following review, work plans were approved by the Government of the Republic of Kazakhstan and used to guide the subsequent phases of the project.

Some delay was encountered during this ratification work because of the restructuring of some state ministries, the managing company (Kazatomprom) and the processing enterprise (UMP) during this period, requiring the repetition of some of the licensing work.

Transportation of nuclear material. The BN-350 fuel was transported without incident 4,649 kilometers by rail from MAEC to UMP in the period from June 25, 2002 to July 3, 2002.

Transportation was potentially the most vulnerable operation of the project from the viewpoint of nuclear material security. Accordingly, the transportation was carried out in secret with restricted information about the route and timing, and with an armed escort at all times. The route and schedule were carefully chosen to minimize the time required for the transportation and the number of stops. The transportation route included six kilometers within the territory of the Republic of Kyrgyzstan and 119 kilometers within the territory of the Russian Federation. At all times, Kazakhstan's armed guards accompanied the train, as permitted by an intergovernmental agreement between the CIS countries, Agreement on transportation of goods and defense products of May 25, 1995. A control center was established, staffed by both UMP representatives and the commanders of the escorting troops, to monitor the transportation and to coordinate security and safety responses in the event of any emergency that may arise.

The KAEC officially notified the IAEA in advance of the transportation in accordance with the Agreement between the IAEA and the Republic of Kazakhstan. After the IAEA determined that appropriate measures were in place, the BN-350 fuel was loaded into specially designed containers, which were then loaded into specialized rail wagons. An IAEA inspector sealed the cargo at the start of the transportation and confirmed that all seals were intact at the end of the transportation. On arrival at UMP, the BN-350 fuel was stored in accordance with the requirements of the legislation of the Republic of Kazakhstan and IAEA standards.

A photographic record was prepared showing different phases of the transportation.

V. Phase Three:
Assessment of the upgrading requirements for the physical protection systems at UMP

The third phase of the project, from October 2003 to June 2004, concerned the requirement for upgrading of the physical protection systems at UMP. These upgrades were a prerequisite to the down-blending of the HEU in order to meet the physical protection requirements for Category 1 nuclear material.

This work included planning the reinforcement of the site security perimeter and improving the physical barriers in the facility areas proposed for down-blending of HEU and the nuclear materials storage areas. New access control equipment was also required, together with additional monitors and alarms.

The NTI project provided funding for a vulnerability assessment and for the technical proposal and improvement plan which described how the physical protection system was to be improved to meet the requirements for Category 1 material, and listed the characteristics and types of equipment required. In addition, the new working instructions which needed to be developed were identified, together with a program of testing and personnel training. The improvement plan also included emergency response planning and a scheme for coordination of appropriate local and national security services.

The technical proposal and improvement plan for the physical protection system was reviewed by both national and international experts, and was then approved by appropriate supervisory organizations of the Republic of Kazakhstan.

VI. Phase Four:
Down-blending of highly enriched BN-350 reactor fuel

This phase started in September 2004 and was completed February 21, 2006. It included modification to buildings at UMP and installation of equipment, commissioning of the new facilities for down-blending of HEU, completion of improvements to the physical protection systems, and down-blending of the HEU contained in the BN-350 fuel. It was the most intensive period of the project.

Installation of the process line for down-blending of the BN-350 fuel, and improvement of the physical protection system, were completed. These tasks were supported by the development of working instructions and obtaining the corresponding permissions and licenses which allowed the process line to be put into operation and the upgrades to the physical protection system to be completed. Special regulations have also been developed for the control, accounting and safety of the HEU during down-blending operations.

Down-blending was controlled by UMP management, who received regular reports on the status of down-blending operations, and internal site transportation between the working zones, storage of nuclear material, laboratory analysis, processing of radioactive wastes, and other aspects of the down-blending facility operations.

Official confirmation by the Republic of Kazakhstan that down-blending of HEU had been completed was sent to the IAEA as the formal notification of the end of the project. This followed regular inspections throughout the project by IAEA staff and the involvement of the IAEA in developing directions, working tasks, and instructions during the project. In addition, all operations were conducted under persistent supervision of the IAEA inspectors.

VII. Conclusion

The most reliable method to reduce the threat of proliferation of nuclear weapons usable materials is their transformation into forms that preclude use in the manufacture of weapons. As a result of the NTI project, 2,897 kg of fresh BN-350 reactor fuel was down-blended by the end of February 2006 and placed into safe storage. Throughout the project the material has remained under IAEA safeguards.

In order to achieve this, new technical facilities have been established at the UMP for the down-blending of HEU and the physical protection systems at the UMP site have been upgraded.

This project has demonstrated the feasibility of developing complex engineering and organizational solutions for down-blending HEU into commercially valuable nuclear material which is not weapons usable. This successful project in Kazakhstan may well prove to be a harbinger of, and a model for, the development of similar projects in other countries.

Chapter 2

GRIM CONSEQUENCES OF NUCLEAR TESTING, AND THE CLOSING OF THE SEMIPALATINSK TEST SITE:

Foundations for Kazakhstan's Firm Stand for a Nuclear-Weapons-Free Future

Los Angeles Times

September 15, 1993

Atom-Test Legacy Shadows
Kazakh Prairie's Calm

Radiation: The Soviets suppressed data on the health effects of over 400 blasts. Experts are meeting today to outline research

By Ian MacWilliam
Special to *The Times*

SARZHAL, Kazakhstan – Kabden Esengarin sits outside in the evening watching his grandchildren play and listening to the wind rustle the poplar trees. Life here on the vast Kazakh steppe south of Siberia seems far removed from the stresses of the 20th Century.

The calm is misleading. For 42 years, the rolling green prairie beyond this village, where horses graze, was the Soviet Union's main test site for atomic bombs. Known simply as the Polygon, the Russian term for firing range, it was shaken by more than 400 nuclear blasts.

Atomic testing ended here in 1991, along with the Soviet Union. But medical authorities are just starting to come to grips with the apparent legacy of the fallout – the increased rates of cancer and birth defects registered here and in other settlements near the uninhabited 7,000-square-mile test site.

"We were told that the Polygon was clean, and the testing would not affect our health," said Esengarin, 74, a retired health official who watched the first bomb explode here in 1949 and remembers the illnesses that followed.

"If somebody died of stomach cancer, we couldn't report that," he said, recalling the obsessive secrecy around the testing. "We had to write down 'stomach problems' or something like that. People from the KGB came to make sure we said nothing more."

With the KGB gone and the region reopened to outsiders, about 100 medical specialists and other researchers from the former Soviet Union, the West and Japan will gather today in Semipalatinsk, the city nearest the Polygon, to outline the first systematic research into the human and ecological damage from the bombs.

Until 1963, nuclear tests were conducted aboveground about 40 miles southwest of Semipalatinsk. When atmospheric blasts were banned by the Limited Test Ban Treaty that year, the explosions here were moved underground.

All this was done with little regard for human safety. Villagers living on the edge of the Polygon and people who worked inside say they were never told that they faced health hazards.

Yano Yeryinba, who now drives a taxi in Semipalatinsk, worked on a government oil-drilling project in the Polygon for 18 months in the 1960s. "When they were setting off an explosion they took us 30 kilometers [19 miles] or so out of the Polygon," said Yeryinba, who reports chronic "stomach problems" and had had an operation. "Two or three hours after the explosion, we came back."

Because Soviet authorities long prohibited doctors from attributing any illness to radiation, the human damage from the fallout is unclear. Kazakh President Nursultan Nazarbayev told a recent conference that his people "still suffer huge losses in connection with nuclear testing."

Statistical estimates belatedly compiled by local physicians in recent years indicate a significant increase in cancers in this region between 1981 and 1991. According to Semipalatinsk's Regional Oncology Center, the number of breast cancer cases per 100,000 inhabitants in that period rose from 13.7 to 23.7, the number of uterine cancer cases from 1.7 to 7.3.

The number of babies with birth defects in Semipalatinsk is 239 per 100,000 live births, compared to 170 per 100,000 in Kazakhstan as a whole, said Dr. Mukhtar Tuleutayev, chief doctor of the regional children's hospital, who declared: "There's a direct connection between children's health and the nuclear testing."

Tuleutayev's efforts in the last years of the Soviet Union to prove such a connection met with frustration. He worked with a team of specialists from the Soviet Radiology Institute in Moscow that did blood analyses in 1989 of people living near the Polygon.

Researchers initially concluded that nuclear radiation had caused immunodeficiency and chromosome aberrations resulting in birth defects, he said. But when the team returned to Moscow, its report was suppressed. It has yet to be published.

In Sarzhal's low mud-brick houses, 12 miles from the Polygon, people are slowly learning the risk to which they have been exposed, but most view it with resignation.

There is a common belief that local people cannot live elsewhere because they have "adapted" to radiation. People tell stories of friends or relatives who moved to Moscow and suddenly fell ill. There may be some basis for this belief, says Tuleutayev, as radiation hardens the artery walls, making the body less adaptable to different climates.

In his wards, Lyuba Terkhova, 5, suffers from bleeding under the skin, and Roshon Nurseitova, 6, has a rare blood disease that causes pains in her legs and stomach. The chief of surgery, Dr. Samat Ospanov, pointed to a mother nursing an infant with immunodeficiency. The baby's fragile skin peels off, and she requires a skin transplant from her mother.

"It's difficult to say whether this could be caused by radiation," Ospanov said. "But when they were setting off nuclear explosions, we had many more children with this problem."

THE TYEE

A FEISTY ONE ONLINE

www.thetyee.ca

July 10, 2006

Silent Bombs in Kazakhstan

Nuclear tragedy worsens with new generation. A special report.

By Carrie-May Siggins

In Zharlanka village in north-eastern Kazakhstan, clusters of people slowly walk towards a small concrete mosque. The village doctor, Kulpan Dyusembayeva, says the girl was 15, the top student in her class. Last week, she was at her desk in the family living room, finishing her homework, when she put down her pen, stood up and walked out the door as if following someone. Her family later found her hanging in a shed a few metres away. It is the third suicide this year, the second of a child in this village of 2,000 people. The previous suicide was a 10-year-old boy.

Zharlanka is roughly 18 kilometers from what was the Semipalatinsk polygon, or test site, in north-eastern Kazakhstan. There, from 1949 to 1989, the Soviet Union tested 456 nuclear and thermonuclear weapons. As a result, cancer rates in the surrounding region are twice the world rate. Physical deformities, mental underdevelopment and heart disease are also common. Most nearby villages have residents with some form of anaemia or skin disease.

Doctors are unsure why these rates are so high. They suspect the cause is small, continual doses of radiation, and genes. Skipping a generation, the grandchildren of those exposed before 1962 are developing an array of serious health problems, from cancer to deformities to schizophrenia. Doctors fear the toll will mount indefinitely as mutated genes are passed from generation to generation.

'Beautiful mushrooms'

On August 29, 1949, Igor Kurchatov, head of the Soviet nuclear program, and three of his generals celebrated in a concrete bunker after detonating the first of what would be 118 atmospheric nuclear weapons tests in the following 13 years.

The first was one of the deadliest. The fallout from that explosion covered the village of Dolon, 31 miles from the site, in radioactive dust. All 800 villagers were exposed to high levels of radiation, and today Dolon has one of the highest rates of cancer in the province. From that day until 1962, when an international treaty banned above-ground testing, the Kazakh government estimates that 200,000 people living in the region had direct exposure to dangerously high levels of radiation. Even when the testing became "safe" and went underground, radioactive gas leaks accompanied nearly 30 per cent of all detonations. The government estimates that a total of 1.2 million people have been affected by the nuclear explosions at the polygon.

Until 1962, preventative measures for citizens living in the area were token at best. Sasha, a sturdy older woman in a blue cotton dress and black babushka, is breaking up the dirt of her bare garden with a shovel. She invites us into her home, and leads us through a large, empty kitchen painted into the back room, where traditional Kazakh rugs are pinned to the walls. She pours us bowls of fresh horse milk and describes being herded into trucks as a child. Soldiers would then take her and her family to makeshift camps. Before a blast, soldiers would tell her that there would be something in the distance, and not to look.

"I can't count how many times I saw them," she says. "We were happy. We saw this beautiful mushroom in the sky. 'Oh look at that,' we would say." Fifteen days later, they would be taken back to their village. After a few years, even this small measure was stopped. Soldiers would simply order Sasha's family to lie on the ground outside of their house and throw a heavy blanket over them as the hydrogen blasts filled the sky.

Secret human study

Sasha is now 60, and a very sick woman, with kidney, liver, stomach, bladder and lung problems. "All the organs of my body are sick," she says. Her oldest son was born mentally underdeveloped. She works as a midwife in this poverty-stricken village, where every second building is an unfinished shell and horses with jutting ribs roam freely, eating weeds. After Kazakh independence, the country experienced what its citizens call "the fall" – a lack of funds to support even the most basic needs of its citizens. In Sarzhal, there was no money to continue construction, so in 1994, it simply stopped. Villagers here are despondent, says Sasha, depressed, and don't bother attempting to restart the construction. As a midwife, Sasha says that she has seen "so many" children damaged, especially in the last few years.

According to one report compiled by the U.S. Department of Energy in 2001, between 1949 and 1963, the Semipalatinsk oblast, or province, had twice the rate of leukemia of other oblasts. The same with thyroid, breast and stomach cancers. The rate was even higher for diseases of the nervous system. From 1982 to 1996, there was another jump in thyroid cancers as the third generations of those exposed were born.

Those numbers are known because, in 1957, a secret medical institution called Brucellosis Dispensary Number 4 was established in Semipalatinsk. Thirty-five scientists housed in this small, concrete building were ordered by Moscow to keep secret medical records of 20,000 people living in heavily contaminated settlements. The sick weren't treated, but studied. Professor Boris Gusev, now head of the Research Institute of Radiation Medicine and Ecology, was a doctor there. "The main reason, our main task," he says, "was to study." To treat them would be to tamper with the experiment.

Long after the effects of radiation were known, the Soviet Union continued to publicly blame the region's high mortality rate on "the poor Kazakh diet." There are some who even believe Semipalatinsk was chosen exactly because it was populated – taking the nuclear experiment out of the lab and into the field. "Semipalatinsk was an experiment of nuclear war on the small scale of the Semi region," says Gusev. "That's the attitude they had. Our only ideology was to counter the U.S., anything to counter the U.S., anything for the mother country."

Soldiers in the dark

The estimated 30,000 soldiers who served on the site during the years of testing, of which only 100 are alive today, were not told by the Soviets of the dangerous levels of radiation. After enlisting, soldiers were forced to sign a confidentiality agreement barring them from telling anyone where they had served. Under Soviet rule, doctors were forbidden to mention radiation in their diagnosis. It wasn't until after the fall of the Soviet Union that soldiers, after being misdiagnosed for years, felt safe telling doctors and families of their exposure.

Meglis Metov, a former soldier and computer engineer, frequently dabs his wet eyes with the corner of a white handkerchief. He's not overcome with emotion, but suffering from an eye condition he blames on watching the blasts. Metov served on the site from 1961 to 1962, "to my bad luck," he says. Knowing that the ban on atmospheric testing loomed near, the military rushed to detonate 14 above-ground nuclear explosions between August and December of 1962. Metov's job was to travel into the "hot zone" one hour after a blast to fix ground cable. Although they understood that radiation could be dangerous, "we never knew about the levels of radiation," he says. "We never had equipment to test the levels."

When they weren't working, Metov and his fellow soldiers enjoyed sitting out on a cliff smoking cigarettes and watching what they called the fireworks in the sky. "We thought it was beautiful," says Metov. One night, they were sitting in their usual spot when the bomb was detonated not atmospherically, but on the ground, closer than any of the young men had expected. "The mushroom was black, and it unfolded," Metov explains. The force of it knocked them onto their backs. "Then the wind changed, and took the whole cloud with it." The black cloud crawled over them, "and took over to our cliff." Immediately, the commanding officer drove the three young soldiers out into the middle of the steppe. They were made to sleep the night with nothing but their T-shirts and shorts. The next day they were given a shower and a glass of vodka, and returned to the site. "They said the cliff was contaminated, but really, we were contaminated ourselves."

Soon after arriving at the site, Metov spent a month in the infirmary with a painful skin condition. "It just began to peel off," he says. He is now an activist fighting for the rights of soldiers who had served at Semipalatinsk. He himself has a host of health problems, including glaucoma, heart and liver disease, and skin conditions.

The new generation

The polygon is now shut down: 7,142 square miles of empty, endless grassland mostly used for study by international scientists. According to the National Nuclear Center in Kazakhstan, 17 per cent of this area is still highly radioactive, although which 17 per cent is still unknown. What makes the discovery of this information urgent is that, although a massive educational campaign in the region has recently curbed the problem, shepherds still graze their flocks on the site. The sheep are then used for meat, and the wool sold in town markets. Villagers use the massive "nuclear lake," a water-filled crater caused by one of the biggest underground blasts, to fish and swim. Although the water isn't considered contaminated, the muddy rim of the lake is. Contaminated materials have travelled far outside the area as well. Until the site was picked bare, scavengers stole copper wire and other scrap metals from the abandoned testing equipment to sell to distributors, spreading the highly radioactive materials into the rest of Kazakhstan, China and Russia.

Kulpan Dyusembayeva sits quietly in the corner, hands folded in her lap, as her husband does most of the talking. When there is a pause, she tells us that she has been Zharlanka's chief doctor for 33 years. "Everyone is sick," she says. There are the child suicides, which some doctors believe are bouts of undiagnosed schizophrenia caused by mutated genes. Schizophrenia is usually first detected when the hormonal changes of puberty begin. The children of villages such as Zharlanka have no one to talk to about what they are experiencing. Therapy and general mental health is still largely unexplored in Kazakhstan. So the children simply act on what comes to them.

And then there is the cancer and heart disease. Dyusembayeva describes how cancer rates in her village have risen in the last five years. It's only May, and already this year six people have died of the disease in this village of 2,000 people. Adults as young as 35 are dying of heart disease. Ninety per cent of villagers have skin conditions. The birth defects in the tiny village are common, and incurable.

'Jelly babies'

Gusev and his researchers at the Institute of Radiology and Oncology believe that illness such as that experienced in Zharlanka is a result of a combination of things. These include stress, malnutrition and high-fat diets. Add to these factors of rural poverty small, continual doses of radiation over a span of decades, and what you get are entire populations critically ill.

As well, many of the grandchildren of those exposed to testing before 1962 are dying at alarming rates, due to what a medical report describes as "radiation-induced mutation in the chromosomes in the sperm and ova." Scientists are surprised to note that these health problems seemed to have skipped a generation. "Children of the second generation, born of the exposed parents, are thousands of times healthier than their exposed parents," says Gusev. "But for some reason, we don't know why, those born from the second generation, their health conditions are hundreds times worse than the second and even the first generation, those initially exposed." Diseases found in the third generation include encephalitis, which causes the infant's cranium to be many times its normal size. Some children are born with scarcely any bones in their arms and legs, leaving only stocking-like limbs of flesh. Locals call them "jelly babies." Other common birth defects include cleft palettes, "rabbit nose," and skin problems.

Gusev says scientists at his institute are working to prove that these genetic deformities are linked to nuclear testing.

Protests and compensation

The Kazakh government compensates those who worked and lived in the area at the time of the initial blasts based on how close they were to "ground zero." Different zones are classified by their contamination levels, and the closer one was, the more money one gets. But for those currently suffering the effects, everyone who applies receives the same treatment, the same amount of money, no matter the severity of their condition. And everyone agrees it is not enough to make a fundamental difference in their lives. The average civilian compensation is around US$60 a month.

In 2003, the United Nations passed a resolution calling for funds to be directed into the Semipalatinsk region. Most medical supplies and equipment in north-eastern Kazakhstan are now donated by foreign countries, such as Japan, which has given millions of dollars in financial and scientific support, as with many other nations such as Holland, the U.S. and France. These countries have also sent scientists to the region regularly to study the effects of radiation. Many villagers complain that after being examined like guinea pigs, there is never anything to show for it. No one is helped; they are not shown the results. Things are simply left the way they've always been.

But the story of Semipalatinsk is also one of hope, and of an awakening democracy. Since the fall of the Soviet Union, NGOs such as Nevada-Semipalatinsk have fought for the rights of those victimized by the nuclear testing. In 1989, tens of thousands of Kazakhs came together to protest the silence surrounding the testing, and two million signed a petition calling for the closing of the site and for the recognition of those who had suffered. In 1991, Kazakhstan's polygon was finally closed. But, although Russia compensates its own citizens for any damage done as a result of testing, it has yet to publicly acknowledge any effects in Kazakhstan.

The Kazakh people are finally reclaiming their history and learning the extent of the damage done by their former Soviet rulers. Through this knowledge they are being empowered to act. But in an era when nuclear weapons are still being produced and countries such as the U.S., North Korea and Iran are threatening to use them as a deterrent or show of power, the story of Semipalatinsk is more vital than ever.

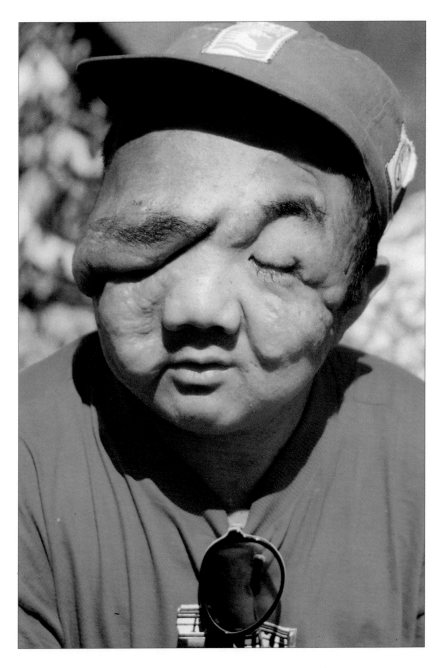

A lifelong burden. Deformities from nuclear radiation are a result of Soviet nuclear weapons testing at Semipalatinsk.

Kazakhstan: Nuclear Testing

On August 29, 1949, the Soviet Union conducted the explosion of its first atomic bomb at the Semipalatinsk nuclear test site in Eastern Kazakhstan. Its power output amounted to 22,000 tons of TNT equivalent.

During the next 40 years, 456 nuclear and thermonuclear explosions were conducted at the test site with the cumulative power output equal to 2,500 bombs dropped on Hiroshima, Japan.

Chrononolgy

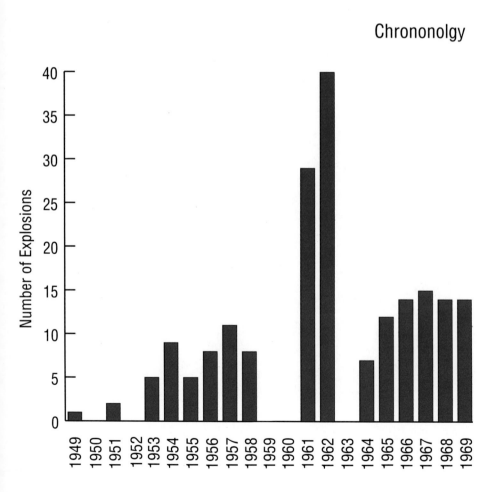

by the Numbers

The testing damaged the lives of 1.5 million people in Kazakhstan. The zone of environmental contamination around the former Semipalatinsk test site spreads over more than 300,000 square kilometers, comparable to the territories of Germany or Italy and equal to more than 10 percent of Kazakhstan's territory.

of Testing

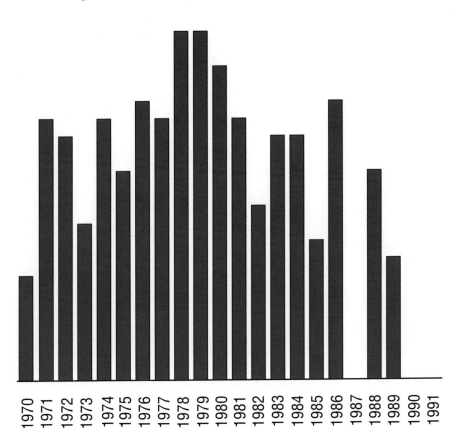

1970 1971 1972 1973 1974 1975 1976 1977 1978 1979 1980 1981 1982 1983 1984 1985 1986 1987 1988 1989 1990 1991

The first Soviet atomic bomb RDS-1, with a yield of 22 kilotons, detonated at the Semipalatinsk test site on August 29, 1949.

One of the 456 Soviet nuclear and thermonuclear explosions at the Semipalatinsk nuclear test site during four decades of testing.

The Soviet military-industrial complex was the master of the Semipalatinsk nuclear test site for more than four decades.

GENERAL INFORMATION

Test Site area ~18500 km²

Foundation date - 08.21.1947
Closure date - 08. 29.1991

First test - 08.29.1949
Last test -10.19.1989

Air tests - 86
Surface tests - 30
Underground tests - 340

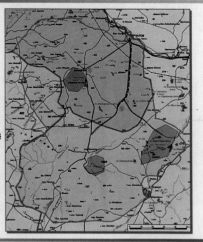

Air 7% · Surface 19% · Underground 74%

in boreholes 29%
in tunnels 45%

■ Air ■ Surface ■ Underground

NUCLEAR FALLOUT PATHS

Surface tests:

① August 29, 1949 – 22 kt
② September 24, 1951 – 38 kt

Thermonuclear Surface Explosion:

③ August 12, 1953 – 400 kt

Surface explosion:

④ August 24, 1956 – 27 kt

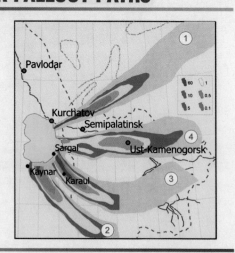

A RS-20 (NATO classification SS-18 "Satan") intercontinental ballistic missile. After independence, Kazakhstan had 104 of these Soviet missiles with 1,040 nuclear warheads aimed at the United States. All were removed from Kazakhstan.

A TU-95M strategic bomber (NATO classification "Bear-A"). Kazakhstan had a squadron of 40 TU-95M bombers armed with tactical cruise missiles with nuclear warheads.

Two of the many victims of nuclear testing at Semipalatinsk.

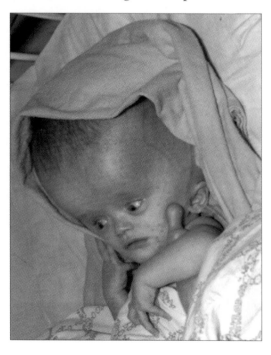

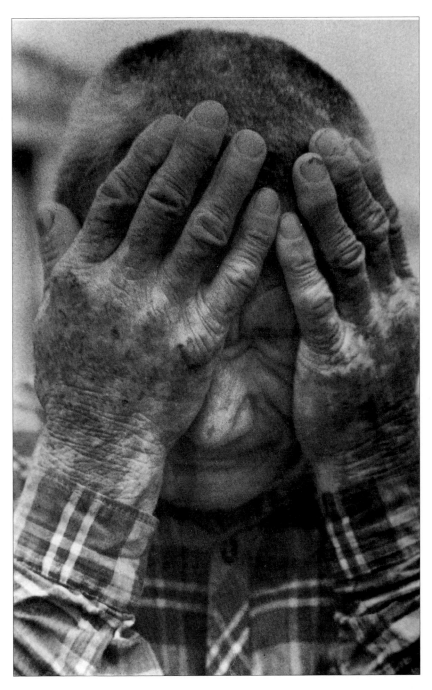

An old man grieves with his people.

"Stop nuclear testing!"

The issue cuts across the ages. Her sign says "No Nuclear War!"

A rally of the Nevada-Semipalatinsk antinuclear movement.—1991

President Nazarbayev: "The test site will be shut down."—1991

Decree #409
of the President of the Kazakh Soviet Socialist Republic on Shutting Down the Semipalatinsk Nuclear Test Site

КАЗАК СОВЕТТІК СОЦИАЛИСТІК РЕСПУБЛИКАСЫ ПРЕЗИДЕНТІНІҢ

ЖАРЛЫҒЫ

УКАЗ

ПРЕЗИДЕНТА КАЗАХСКОЙ СОВЕТСКОЙ СОЦИАЛИСТИЧЕСКОЙ РЕСПУБЛИКИ

Семей ядролық сынақ полигонын жабу туралы

О закрытии Семипалатинского испытательного ядерного полигона

Қазақ ССР=інің терри
бері ядролық қару сынау ж
де онда 500-ге жуық ядрол
адамдардың денсаулығы мен

Қазақ ССР-і ССРО мен
теңдікті қамтамасыз еткен
борышын орындағанын ескер
рына құлақ асып, ҚАУЛЫ ЕТ

1. Семей ядролық сын

2. Қазақ ССР Министр
мен, ССРО Атом энергетика
келісе отырып, Семей сына
ми=зерттеу орталығы етіп
және ғылыми=зерттеу жұмыс
әзірлеп, бекітсін.

3. 1949 жылдан 1962
тар жүргізу кезінде Семей
саулығына нұқсан келтірі
бірге Қазақ ССР=інің зард
шері мен тәртібі белгілен

4. Қазақ ССР Министрлер Кабинеті республика территориясын-
да ядролық жарылыстар жасауға қатысты одақтық министрліктермен
және ведомстволармен бірге Семей, Қарағанды және Павлодар облыс-
тарының сынақ полигонына іргелес аудандарының әлеуметтік=эконо -
микалық дамуының, олардағы халықтың тұрмыс жағдайларын және олар-
ға медициналық қызмет көрсетілуін жақсартудың бағдарламасын бекітсін, аталған мақсаттарға тиісті одақтық көздерден қаржылар қатыс-
тырылсын.

Осы Жарлық қабылданған кезінен бастап күшіне енеді.

Қазақ
Советтік Социалистік Республикасының   Н. НАЗАРБАЕВ
Президенті

Алматы, 1991 жылғы тамыздың 29-ы.
№ 409

Decree #409

Since 1949, nuclear arms tests were conducted on the territory of the Semipalatinsk region of the Kazakh SSR. Around 500 nuclear explosions were carried out which caused damage to the health and lives of thousands of people.

Taking into account that the Kazakh SSR has fulfilled its duty vis-à-vis the creation of a nuclear potential that has ensured the strategic parity between the USSR and the USA, and taking into consideration the demands of the people of the Republic,

I RESOLVE:
1. To shut down the Semipalatinsk nuclear test site.
2. That the Cabinet of Ministers of the Kazakh SSR, in coordination with the Ministry of Defense of the USSR and the Ministry of Atomic Energy and Industry of the USSR, transform the Semipalatinsk test site into a Union-Republic research center and develop and approve its status and a list of main directions of scientific research.
3. Taking into account that during the air and ground tests in the period from 1949 through 1962, harm was done to the health of the people in areas bordering the Semipalatinsk nuclear test site, to define jointly with the agencies of the Union the scale and mechanisms of compensating the citizens of the Kazakh SSR who have suffered such harm.
4. That the Cabinet of Ministers of the Kazakh SSR, together with the ministries and agencies of the Union that were involved in conducting nuclear explosions on the territory of the Republic, approve a program of social and economic development to improve living standards and healthcare of the people in the districts of the Semipalatinsk, Karaganda and Pavlodar regions bordering the test site, to be funded from the Union budget.

This Decree enters into force from the moment of its signing.

Nursultan Nazarbayev
President of the Kazakh Soviet Socialist Republic

Almaty, August 29, 1991

The nuclear era ends in Kazakhstan as the gates slam shut at
Semipalatinsk.

United Nations

The situation in the Semipalatinsk region remains critical

Kofi Annan, United Nations Secretary General

Excerpted from the report by the UN Secretary General to the 60th Session of the United Nations General Assembly, "Humanitarian assistance and rehabilitation for selected countries and regions" (A/60/302), of August 25, 2005.

Kazakhstan

By its resolution 57/101, on international cooperation and coordination for the human and ecological rehabilitation and economic development of the Semipalatinsk region of Kazakhstan, the General Assembly requested the Secretary General to report at its sixtieth session on progress made in the implementation of that resolution. This report summarizes actions undertaken in the past three years by the United Nations system, the Government of Kazakhstan and the international community in the Semipalatinsk region, and concludes that the efforts have not been sufficient to mitigate the suffering caused by years of nuclear testing.

Economic and social conditions

The Semipalatinsk nuclear testing area is a lingering consequence of the Cold War. Between 1949 and 1989, 468 nuclear tests, including 125 above-ground tests, were conducted in this

81

18,500 km2 polygon. Although this area was developed and used exclusively by the Soviet Union, the burden of dealing with the consequences fell on Kazakhstan when it gained independence in the early 1990s.

This burden is significant: an estimated 1,323,000 people were negatively affected by the tests, and many continue to suffer today. While the national mortality rate in 2003 from oncological diseases was 126 per 100,000 people, the rate was 163 and 189 per 100,000 people, respectively, in the Pavlodar and East Kazakhstan oblasts, where the nuclear test site was located.

Recognizing the international responsibilities connected to Semipalatinsk and the severity of the health, environmental and social problems there, the General Assembly adopted four resolutions between 1997 and 2002 calling on the international community to assist the Government of Kazakhstan in its efforts to overcome those problems.

In September 1999, an international conference on Semipalatinsk was organized in Tokyo to consider the Semipalatinsk Relief and Region Rehabilitation Program. The program consisted of 38 impact-oriented projects valued at $43 million for relief and rehabilitation in five main areas: health, environment and ecology, economic recovery, humanitarian support, and information and advocacy. In response, the international donor community pledged more than $20 million in assistance. Since then, numerous projects have been supported by the Government of Kazakhstan and the international community to help rehabilitate the region. Although much has been accomplished, the severity of the problems has thus far outweighed the efforts to resolve them.

Thus, in its resolution 57/101, the General Assembly stressed again the need for continuing international attention to address the problems of the Semipalatinsk region, further urged the international community to provide assistance and invited all Member States to share their knowledge and experience in order to contribute to the rehabilitation and economic development of the Semipalatinsk region.

Institutional framework for assistance to Semipalatinsk

Prior to the Tokyo conference in 1999, the Government in Kazakhstan formed an interministerial commission to develop a comprehensive plan of action and secure donor funding for Semipalatinsk. Although that commission presented a list of high-priority projects and secured funding from the donor community in Tokyo, implementation of the program has been somewhat fragmentary in nature, due to insufficient financial resources to tackle numerous high-priority problems simultaneously, high turnover among responsible staff members, unfulfilled commitments by donors, numerous smaller ad hoc projects being undertaken by local bodies and nongovernmental organizations outside the main program, etc.

Partly because of those problems and partly due to the growing capacities and prosperity of Kazakhstan stemming from international investments and oil sales during the past six years, donor interest and assistance to Semipalatinsk has waned in recent years.

In an effort to revive interest and to better coordinate Semipalatinsk activities, the Kazakhstan Ministry of Foreign Affairs and UNDP organized a local donor meeting in Almaty in February 2004 to take stock of what had been accomplished, set priorities for further actions, and present additional high-priority projects to the donor community. The donor community indicated that with a vibrant and growing economy and significant State resources, the Government needed to take the lead in setting the agenda for Semipalatinsk, coordinating assistance and demonstrating its commitment through supporting rehabilitation efforts with State resources.

In follow up to that meeting, the Government developed a new program for the period 2005-2007 to address solutions for problems of the former Semipalatinsk nuclear test site.

Donor assistance to the Semipalatinsk region

Through the 1999 Tokyo conference, more than $20 million was pledged by the international community, including the Governments of Japan, the United Kingdom of Great Britain and Northern Ireland and Switzerland, the World Bank, United Nations agencies, Counterpart International and the International Federation of Red Cross and Red Crescent Societies (ICRC). Most pledges were received, but were considerably less than what is needed and some pledges remain unfulfilled.

This section provides a summary of progress made in implementing the Semipalatinsk Relief and Rehabilitation Program since the last report to the General Assembly in July 2002. Unfortunately, most donor programs are now coming or have already come to an end, despite serious problems in the areas of health, environmental degradation and economic development. More important, there are no indications that the trend of reduced support will end. Fewer organizations are offering support and the magnitude of support is considerably smaller.

It should be noted that nongovernmental organizations and local authorities independently implement projects, and thus the information provided here may not provide a complete picture of all assistance.

Health sector

The Japanese Government has supported a major project on the improvement of the regional health-care system in the Semipalatinsk region, which will end in 2005. It provides medical assistance to help improve health checks, diagnosis of illnesses, data processing for systemic studies, etc.

The European Commission, through its Technical Assistance to the Commonwealth of Independent States (TACIS) Program, is implementing an institution-building project to improve women's awareness of their reproductive health rights, train medical personnel on the human rights of women, introduce the concept of low-risk pregnancy and promote intervention-free childbirth. TACIS will also fund a nuclear safety project on the theme "Support for implementing an aero-gamma survey of the Semipalatinsk test site".

UNICEF has supported various initiatives, covering areas such as developing child friendly curriculums, promoting improved parenting skills, training trainers for doctors and nurses, and working with children with special needs to develop alternatives to institutionalization. UNICEF intends to continue developing peer education and life skills based health education in cooperation with nongovernmental organizations (NGOs).

The United States Agency for International Development is implementing a community-oriented primary care project in association with the American International Health Alliance. This project is based on a model family medicine centre in Astana. Local clubs offer a wide range of health education training, counseling and other health-related activities.

The National Red Crescent Society (RCS) of Kazakhstan is implementing three projects in the health sector focusing on tuberculosis prevention, safe motherhood and community-based primary care in rural areas and villages. These projects have been under way for four years and will continue for another two years, with support from the Japanese Red Cross. The RCS also works to raise public awareness on and improve public preparedness for emergencies, and currently supports two projects on the themes "Public confidence", which includes training on emergency responses, and "Mitigation", which includes clearing burnt wood and planting pine trees.

Finally, two projects have recently been finalized, on the themes "Rights of women and social partnership" and "Voice-Protection of voters' rights", which are financed by the European Union through the European Initiative for Democracy and Human Rights.

Humanitarian sector

The Government of Switzerland recently completed a project targeting vulnerable groups, in which support was given to small projects in the amount of $20,000. Those grants also targeted vulnerable groups by, for example, supplying orphanages with equipment such as laundry machines, computers, etc.

The Canadian International Development Agency, through the Canada Fund for Local Initiatives, supported two small projects on sustainable agricultural development implemented by the "Umit Tani" Center for children, orphans and invalids in Semipalatinsk city.

Environmental sector

The United Kingdom Department for International Development is currently completing an environmental project on the theme "Preparation and implementation of a participatory land use plan for the Semipalatinsk test site". This project aims to develop and implement a participatory land use plan for areas that are safe for people and their animals. The plan will be developed in conjunction with local inhabitants so that it can be applied through present administrative structures based in the East Kazakhstan, Karaganda and Pavlodar oblasts.

The Organization for Security and Cooperation in Europe (OSCE) makes scientific data from environmental mapping of residential and public premises in towns adjacent to the Semipalatinsk nuclear test site available in a user-friendly way. In 2005, OSCE is conducting a summer camp for teenagers from villages near the test site to raise awareness about the environmental situation and sustainable development.

Economic sector

The UNDP Semipalatinsk program was funded by the Government of Japan, which contributed $1.1 million through the Trust Fund for the Semipalatinsk Relief and Rehabilitation

Program, a fund created by UNDP in response to United Nations resolutions calling for international assistance. This program, which ends in 2005, included three sub-projects: microcredit for women, small grants for nongovernmental and community-based organizations, and business advisory services. According to an independent evaluation conducted in 2004, this program made substantial progress in helping to alleviate poverty and raise living standards among targeted groups such as women, small-scale entrepreneurs and rural people.

Priorities for further action

In 2005, the Government of Kazakhstan is launching a program to address the problems of the former Semipalatinsk nuclear test site during the period 2005-2007. The main goal is to improve the ecological, economic, medical and social factors affecting the living standards of population in the region. The expected results are (a) a reduction in morbidity rates; and (b) a more secure situation with regard to radiation, which would be met by undertaking activities in the areas of medical rehabilitation; radiological assessment and security; social infrastructure development; and scientific and technical diversification.

The Government of Kazakhstan is expected to provide KZT 2.47 billion (approximately $18.9 million) to finance this program. Because it is a State program, it outlines only activities and support from the Government itself and does not indicate what role other actors such as donors, nongovernmental organizations and the private sector could play. The program could be strengthened by including those actors and providing measures to better coordinate their activities.

Conclusion

The situation in the Semipalatinsk region remains critical with more than 1.3 million people still suffering from the effects of almost 40 years of nuclear tests. The Semipalatinsk polygon has yet to be secured, the local economy is still suffering from the collapse of the Soviet Union, and high morbidity and mortality rates illustrate the high price paid by local people for this legacy of the cold war.

The Government of Kazakhstan and the international community have made some efforts to ameliorate these problems from the days of the Soviet Union. The Government has implemented numerous programs and has developed a program to address the problems of the former Semipalatinsk nuclear test site during the period 2005-2007. The donor community has delivered a substantial amount of assistance since the Tokyo conference in 1999. However, much remains to be done. Member States, in partnership with the Government of Kazakhstan, should strengthen their efforts to assist the people of Semipalatinsk.

In implementing the new program, the Government of Kazakhstan will be able to provide much-needed assistance in the areas of medicine, radiology, science and social welfare. Under the umbrella of this program, the Government also has the opportunity to renew its efforts to coordinate assistance from State resources and the international community. That could be done through establishing a multi-stakeholder coordination mechanism that includes relevant Government ministries, donors, local governments and civil society organizations. The Government of Kazakhstan may call on the United Nations Resident Coordinator and UNDP in Kazakhstan to assist in the effort.

With the Government taking a stronger role in delivering and coordinating assistance, Member States should take complementary actions. In particular, donors and members of the Commonwealth of Independent States must continue to recognize their special obligations to the people of Semipalatinsk, whose suffering stems from the cold war. Member States should first and foremost fulfill all previous pledges, and second, consider what additional expertise and/or resources they could offer to lessen the suffering in Semipalatinsk.

The recent economic prosperity experienced by Kazakhstan is insufficient to resolve the deeply rooted and highly technical problems of radioactive contamination in the Semipalatinsk region. The Government of Kazakhstan is demonstrating its commitment to Semipalatinsk with its new program. With assistance, and in partnership with other Member States, this commitment could produce better results than those that have been achieved thus far.

 General Assembly

Dist. General
29 March 2006

Sixth session

Resolution, adopted by the General Assembly

International cooperation and coordination for the human and ecological rehabilitation and economic development of the Semipalatinsk region of Kazakhstan

Approved on December 22, 2005

The General Assembly,

Recalling its resolutions 52/169 M of 16 December 1997, 53/1 H of 16 November 1998, 55/44 of 27 November 2000 and 57/101 of 25 November 2002,

Welcoming the report of the Secretary General,

Recognizing that the Semipalatinsk nuclear testing ground, inherited by Kazakhstan and closed in 1991, remains a matter of serious concern for the people and Government of Kazakhstan with regard to the long-term nature of its consequences for the lives and health of the people, especially children and other vulnerable groups, as well as for the environment of the region,

Taking into consideration the results of the international conference on the problems of the Semipalatinsk region, held in Tokyo in 1999, which have promoted the effectiveness of the assistance provided to the population of the region,

Recognizing the important role of national development policies and strategies in the rehabilitation of the Semipalatinsk region, and taking note with satisfaction of the elaboration of the Kazakhstan national program entitled 'Complex solution of the former Semipalatinsk nuclear test site problems for 2005-2007',

Recognizing also the contribution of different organizations of the United Nations system, donor States, intergovernmental and nongovernmental organizations to humanitarian assistance and to the implementation of the projects aimed at the rehabilitation of the region and the role of the Government of Kazakhstan in this regard,

Recognizing further the challenges Kazakhstan faces in the rehabilitation of the Semipalatinsk region, in particular in the context of the efforts by the Government of Kazakhstan to ensure an effective and timely achievement of the Millennium Development Goals,

Taking note of the need for know-how in minimizing and mitigating radiological, health, socio-economic, psychological and environmental problems in the Semipalatinsk region,

Taking into account that many international programs in the Semipalatinsk region have been completed whereas serious social, economic and ecological problems continue to exist,

Conscious that the international community should continue to pay due attention to the issue of the human, ecological and socio-economic dimensions of the situation in the Semipalatinsk region,

Emphasizing the importance of support by donor States and international development organizations for the efforts by Kazakhstan to improve the social, economic and environmental situation in the Semipalatinsk region,

1. *Takes note* of the report of the Secretary General and the information about the measures taken to solve the health, ecological, economic and humanitarian problems and to meet the needs of the Semipalatinsk region;

2. *Welcomes and recognizes* the important role of the Government of Kazakhstan in providing domestic resources to help meet the needs of the Semipalatinsk region, including for the implementation of the Kazakhstan national pro-

gram entitled 'Complex solution of the former emipalatinsk nuclear test site problems for 2005-2007';

3. *Calls upon* the international community, including all Member States, in particular donor States, and United Nations institutions to continue to support Kazakhstan in addressing the challenges of the rehabilitation of the Semipalatinsk region and its population, taking additional actions, including by facilitating the implementation of the Kazakhstan national program on addressing the problems of the former Semipalatinsk nuclear testing ground in a comprehensive manner, and stresses the importance of the regional cooperation in this regard;

4. *Urges* the international community to provide assistance to Kazakhstan in the formulation and implementation of special programs and projects of treatment and care for the affected population as well as in the efforts to ensure economic growth and sustainable development in the Semipalatinsk region;

5. *Calls upon* all States, relevant multilateral financial organizations and other entities of the international community, including non-governmental organizations, to share their knowledge and experience in order to contribute to the human and ecological rehabilitation and economic development of the Semipalatinsk region;

6. *Invites* the Secretary General to pursue a consultative process, with the participation of interested States and relevant United Nations agencies, on modalities for mobilizing the necessary support to seek appropriate solutions to the problems and needs of the Semipalatinsk region, including those prioritized in the report of the Secretary General;

7. *Calls upon* the Secretary General to continue his efforts to enhance world public awareness of the problems and needs of the Semipalatinsk region;

8. *Requests* the Secretary General to report to the General Assembly at its sixty-third session, under a separate sub-item, on the progress made in the implementation of the present resolution.

Chapter 3

KAZAKHSTAN'S NUCLEAR DISARMAMENT AND NONPROLIFERATION COOPERATION WITH THE UNITED STATES:

A Global Model for a Safer World

Kazakhstan: A Nation Frees Itself of Weapons of Mass Destruction Legacy

August 29, 1991	President Nursultan Nazarbayev of the Kazakh Soviet Socialist Republic issues a decree shutting down the Semipalatinsk Nuclear Test Site, a full four months before the Soviet Union collapses.
December 16, 1991	The Republic of Kazakhstan declares its independence.
December 26, 1991	Kazakhstan and the USA establish full diplomatic relations. The issue of the fate of the nuclear arsenal in Kazakhstan is of paramount priority for leaders of both countries.
December 30, 1991	The Soviet Union formally ceases to exist. Kazakhstan inherits the world's fourth largest nuclear arsenal, including 1,040 nuclear warheads for intercontinental ballistic missiles (ICBMs) of 1 megaton TNT-equivalent each, 104 RS-20 ICBMs (NATO designation SS-18 "Satan"), as well as a squadron of 40 TU-95 heavy bombers armed with Kh-55 air-land cruise missiles (or ALCMs) (NATO designation AS-15A 'Kent') with 370 tactical nuclear warheads.

May 23, 1992	Kazakhstan signs Lisbon Protocol to the Treaty between the United States of America and the Union of Soviet Socialist Republics on the Reduction and Limitation of Strategic Offensive Arms (START I Treaty), by which it renounces possession of nuclear weapons and accepts obligations to ensure nonproliferation of nuclear weapons.
July 2, 1992	Kazakhstan's Parliament ratifies START I Treaty.
January 14, 1993	Kazakhstan signs the Convention on the Prohibition of the Development, Production, Stockpiling and Use of Chemical Weapons and on their Destruction.
December 13, 1993	Kazakhstan's Parliament ratifies the Nuclear Nonproliferation Treaty. On the same day, in Almaty, President Nursultan Nazarbayev and U.S. Vice President Albert Gore sign the Framework Agreement opening the way toward implementation of the Cooperative Threat Reduction Program (Nunn-Lugar program) in Kazakhstan.
February 14, 1994	President Nursultan Nazarbayev presents ratification documents to President Bill Clinton in Washington, DC, by which Kazakhstan formally accedes to the Nuclear

Nonproliferation Treaty as a non-nuclear-weapon state.

February 1994	Kazakhstan joins the International Atomic Energy Agency (IAEA).
	All 40 TU-95 heavy bombers are removed from Kazakhstan to Russia.
November 1994	Five hundred eighty-one kilograms (1,278 pounds) of highly enriched uranium are removed to the United States from the Ulba Metallurgy Plant in north-eastern Kazakhstan through a joint Kazakhstan-U.S. secret operation code-named Project Sapphire. This material, left at Ulba from the time of nuclear fuel production for Soviet submarines, would have been enough to produce 20-25 nuclear warheads.
December 1994	The United States of America, the United Kingdom of Great Britain and Northern Ireland and the Russian Federation, the states depositories of the NPT Treaty, sign the Memorandum on Security Assurances with Kazakhstan, Belarus and Ukraine, as countries who have renounced nuclear weapons. In short order, France and China, two other nuclear weapons states, provide similar guarantees to Kazakhstan.

April 1995	All 1,040 nuclear warheads for ICBMs and all 370 nuclear warheads for ALCMs are removed from Kazakhstan to Russia.
May 1995	The last nuclear device is destroyed at the Semipalatinsk Nuclear Test Site, after being left there since 1990.
September 1996	Kazakhstan becomes one of the first signatories to the Comprehensive Nuclear Test Ban Treaty.
September 1996	All 104 ICBMs are removed from Kazakhstan to Russia for destruction, three years ahead of schedule required by the START I Treaty.
October 1997	The UN General Assembly approves the first resolution calling on member states to provide assistance to regions of Kazakhstan which suffered from nuclear testing.
September 1999	All 148 ICBM silos are destroyed in four regions across Kazakhstan, including 61 silos at Derzhavinsk, 61 at Zhangyz-Tobe, 14 test silos at Semipalatinsk Nuclear Test Site, and 12 test silos at Leninsk.
March 2000	Kazakhstan ratifies the Chemical Weapons Convention. Kazakhstan becomes the 132nd State Party to the Convention on 22 April 2000, thirty days after depositing its instrument of ratification with the Secretary General of the United Nations.

July 2000	The last test tunnel is destroyed at the Degelen mountain complex at the Semipalatinsk test site. A total of 181 tunnels and 13 unused test holes were destroyed at the test site.
September 2000	The capacity of the world's largest anthrax production and weaponization facility at Stepnogorsk is eliminated. This facility had a capacity to produce 300 metric tons of anthrax agent during a 7-month war-time mobilization period.
July 2001	The joint Kazakhstan-U.S. project concludes at BN-350 fast-breeder reactor in Aktau whose aim was the security of more than 3,200 kilograms (7,250 pounds) of weapons-grade plutonium, enough to produce 400 nuclear bombs. The reactor had been shut down for several years before that.
January 2002	A joint Kazakhstan-U.S. project of government-private partnership starts separating low-enriched uranium from uranium concentrate using a unique technology developed at the Ulba Metallurgy Plant for commercial sale. Fifty high-tech jobs are created.
February 2002	The joint project between the Nuclear Threat Initiative, the Kazatomprom national nuclear company of Kazakhstan, the Ulba Metallurgical Plant and the Nonproliferation

	Support Center begins to securely transport fresh highly enriched uranium fuel from BN-350 reactor and blend it down at Ulba.
May 2002	Kazakhstan is accepted into the Nuclear Suppliers Group, which unites 40 nations and sets principles of export controls in nuclear-related trade.
August 2003	President Nazarbayev awards Order of Dostyk of First Degree, Kazakhstan's highest award for foreigners, to former Senator Sam Nunn and Senator Richard Lugar (R-IN) in recognition of their outstanding contribution to Kazakhstan's disarmament and strengthening of global security.
December 2004	Kazakhstan and the USA sign an amendment to the Framework Agreement on cooperation in nonproliferation of weapons of mass destruction which moved the two nations towards a new level of cooperation in fighting the spread of biological weapons and the threat of bioterrorism. The amendment raised the level of U.S. funding by approximately US$35 million for biological weapons proliferation prevention projects in Kazakhstan, a cooperative biological research program, securing dangerous pathogens and strains by strengthening biosafety and biosecurity at facilities, and other activities.

April 2005	The United States Senate Unanimously adopts Resolution 122, Recognizing the historic efforts of the Republic of Kazakhstan to reduce the threat of weapons of mass destruction through cooperation in the Nunn-Lugar/Cooperative Threat Reduction Program, and celebrating the 10th anniversary of the removal of all nuclear weapons from the territory of Kazakhstan.
September 2005	In addition to all twelve United Nation counter-terrorism conventions, Kazakhstan accedes to the International Convention for the Suppression of Acts of Nuclear Terrorism.
December 2005	The United Nations General Assembly unanimously adopts a resolution calling upon the international community to continue to support Kazakhstan in addressing the challenges of the rehabilitation of the Semipalatinsk region and its population, taking additional actions, including by facilitating the implementation of the Kazakhstan national program on addressing the problems of the former Semipalatinsk nuclear testing ground in a comprehensive manner.
February 2006	The joint Kazatomprom-NTI project on secure transportation of fresh highly enriched uranium fuel from BN-350 reactor and its downblending at

UMP is completed. Almost three tons of highly enriched uranium, enough to produce two dozen nuclear bombs, were downblendedand turned into low enriched uranium usable only in peaceful purposes.

May 2006	Kazakhstan and the USA sign an agreement under the Second Line of Defense program of the U.S. Department of Energy calling for greater cooperation in preventing illicit trafficking of nuclear materials through the supply and deployment of special radiation detection equipment. The agreement provides for the expansion of U.S. financing of WMD infrastructure elimination projects in Kazakhstan up to 158 million U.S. dollars.
July 2006	Kazakhstan supports the Global Initiative to Combat Nuclear Terrorism announced by Russia and the USA.
	The United States House of Representatives unanimously adopts Resolution 905, congratulating Kazakhstan on the 15th anniversary of the closure of the world's second largest nuclear test site in the Semipalatinsk region. The resolution notes that "Kazakhstan's leadership and cooperation with the United States on nonproliferation matters is a model for other countries to follow."

THE WHITE HOUSE

WASHINGTON

December 26, 1991

The Honorable Nursultan A. Nazarbayev
President of the Republic of Kazakhstan
Almaty, Kazakhstan

Dear Mr. President,

In view of the historic changes that have taken place in your country and the termination of the Union which bound together the republics of the former Soviet Union, I am pleased to inform you that United States Government recognize Kazakhstan as an independent state.

Over the past several months we have carried on an extensive and constructive dialogue concerning issues critical to the interests of both the United States and Kazakhstan, as well as the entire world. We have agreed that, during and after this period of transition, Russia, Ukraine, Kazakhstan, and Belarus must ensure safe, responsible, and reliable control over nuclear weapons under a single authority. We have welcomed your commitment to ensure the safety, security, and accelerated destruction of nuclear weapons on your territory, and have offered our assistance in that process. You and we have agreed that Kazakhstan must put into place a legislative and institutional regime to prevent the proliferation and export of weapons of mass destruction and other destabilizing military technologies, as well as the know-how to make them. We have welcomed the commitment of Kazakhstan to implement fully the START and CFE treaties, to join the NPT as a non-nuclear state, and to agree to full-scope IAEA safeguards.

You have also expressed the firm commitment of Kazakhstan to the democratic values and specific obligations embodied in all CSCE agreements, including the Helsinki Agreement and Charter of Paris. We have welcomed your determination to move rapidly toward the creation of a market economy in Kazakhstan. You have further assured us of your commitment to fulfill the treaty and other obligations of the former USSR.

In view of your affirmation of all of these commitments to Secretary Baker, I am pleased to propose that our two countries conduct full diplomatic relations with permanent missions. It is my intention to name an ambassador to Kazakhstan in the near future, and I invite you to indicate your plans with respect to an ambassador to the United States. I look forward to your response agreeing to these arrangements and to the continued development of cordial and productive relations between Kazakhstan and the United States of America.

Finally, I would like to invite you to visit Washington in the first part of 1992 so that we can review together the many important issues.

Sincerely,

George H.W. Bush

At the conclusion of this important meeting, we – the President of the United States and the President of the Republic of Kazakhstan – have resolved to develop friendly, cooperative relations between our countries and peoples, and to work together to strengthen international peace and stability.

Kazakhstan and the United States favor an early ratification and implementation of the START Treaty as an important guarantor of maintaining global stability. Reaffirming its commitment to peace and security, Kazakhstan shall, at the earliest possible time, accede to the Treaty on the Nonproliferation of Nuclear Weapons as a non-nuclear state, while preserving the right to control over the non-use and reductions of the nuclear weapons temporarily deployed on its territory. Kazakhstan guarantees to carry out the elimination of all types of nuclear weapons, including strategic offensive arms, within the seven-year period provided for in the START Treaty. The United States welcomes these steps and shall take necessary measures to assist Kazakhstan in this matter. Kazakhstan and the United States agree on the need to establish effective national control over nonproliferation of the weapons of mass destruction and associated technologies to third countries.

The United States and Kazakhstan will work to strengthen international security on the basis of lower and more stable levels of armaments among all nations.

Excerpt from the Joint Declaration by President George H.W. Bush and President Nursultan Nazarbayev on relations between the United States and Kazakhstan, May 19, 1992

The Washington Post

May 22, 1992

Liquidating a Nuclear Inheritance

The urgent and delicate task of disposing of the nuclear arms of the three nations other than Russia that inherited the Soviet strategic arsenal is notably closer to completion as a result of the Washington trip of Nursultan Nazarbayev, president of Kazakhstan. His huge Central Asian country found itself in possession, though not in actual command, of more than 1,000 missile warheads and 370 aircraft bombs. This raised the specter that he would hang on to these weapons for political bargaining and in so doing spoil arms control and quicken proliferation. But from Russia, China and, now, the United States, he has gained the security and other assurances that let him move toward the right position in this crucial policy area.

Kazakhstan, along with Ukraine and Belarus, now pledges to accept its share of the disarmament obligations of the START treaty. That means turning back strategic weapons to be dismantled by Russia; battlefield weapons are already returned. Kazakhstan is also assuming the no-proliferation obligations of the Nuclear Nonproliferation Treaty. In return, it is to slip under the protective umbrella the nuclear powers promise to raise over non-nuclear treaty signers. It is also moving to improve its security ties with Russia and other states of the former Soviet Union, to remove possible bones of contention between it and nuclear China and to move into a broad pattern of cooperative relations with Washington and the West.

The American Government has rightly given high priority to updating START and keeping that treaty and the nonproliferation treaty on track. But in the course of seeing to the world,s first instances of denuclearization, in Kazakhstan, Ukraine and Belarus, the United States has come under their strong insistence to meet its own nonproliferation treaty commitments by halting nuclear testing. In Washington President Nazarbayev underlined the point; he speaks knowingly and strongly of the immense public health and environmental costs that Soviet testing inflicted on Kazakhstan. A testing moratorium is running throughout the old Soviet Union and France.

The nonproliferation treaty was always meant to involve a match of obligations: abstinence by nuclear have-nots, progressive limiting of arms and options by haves. Fortunately, warming world circumstances make it safe and plausible for Americans to do their part.

Protocol to the Treaty
Between the United States of America and the Union of Soviet Socialist Republics on the Reduction and Limitation of Strategic Offensive Arms

The Republic of Byelarus, the Republic of Kazakhstan, the Russian Federation, Ukraine, and the United States of America, hereinafter referred to as the Parties,

Reaffirming their support for the Treaty Between the United States of America and the Union of Soviet Socialist Republics on the Reduction and Limitation of Strategic Offensive Arms of July 31, 1991, hereinafter referred to as the Treaty,

Recognizing the altered political situation resulting from the replacement of the former Union of Soviet Socialist Republics with a number of independent states,

Recalling the commitment of the member states of the Commonwealth of Independent States that the nuclear weapons of the former Union of Soviet Socialist Republics will be maintained under the safe, secure, and reliable control of a single unified authority,

Desiring to facilitate implementation of the Treaty in this altered situation,

Have agreed as follows:

ARTICLE I

The Republic of Byelarus, the Republic of Kazakhstan, the Russian Federation, and Ukraine, as successor states of the former Union of Soviet Socialist Republic in connection with the Treaty, shall assume the obligations of the former Union of Soviet Socialist Republics under the Treaty.

ARTICLE II

The Republic of Byelarus, the Republic of Kazakhstan, the Russian Federation, and Ukraine shall make such arrangements among themselves as are required to implement the Treaty's limits and restrictions; to allow functioning of the verification provisions of the Treaty equally and consistently throughout the territory of the Republic of Byelarus, the Republic of Kazakhstan, the Russian Federation, and Ukraine; and to allocate costs.

ARTICLE III

1. For purposes of Treaty implementation, the phrase, "Union of Soviet Socialist Republics" shall be interpreted to mean the Republic of Byelarus, the Republic of Kazakhstan, the Russian Federation, and Ukraine.
2. For purposes of Treaty implementation, the phrase, "national territory," when used in the Treaty to refer to the Union of Soviet Socialist Republics, shall be interpreted to mean the combined national territories of the Republic of Byelarus, the Republic of Kazakhstan, the Russian Federation, and Ukraine.
3. For inspections and continuous monitoring activities on the territory of the Republic of Byelarus, the Republic of Kazakhstan, the Russian Federation, or Ukraine, that state shall provide communications from the inspection site or continuous monitoring site to the Embassy of the United States in the respective capital.
4. For purposes of Treaty implementation, the embassy of the Inspecting Party referred to in Section XVI of the Protocol on Inspections and Continuous Monitoring Activities Relating to the Treaty between the United States of America and the Union of Soviet Socialist Republics on the Reduction and Limitation of Strategic Offensive Arms shall be construed to be the embassy of the respective state in Washington or the embassy of the United States of America in the respective capital.
5. The working languages for Treaty activities shall be English and Russian.

ARTICLE IV

Representatives of the Republic of Byelarus, the Republic of Kazakhstan, the Russian Federation, and Ukraine will participate in the Joint Compliance and Inspection Commission on a basis to be worked out consistent with Article I of this Protocol.

ARTICLE V

The Republic of Byelarus, the Republic of Kazakhstan, and Ukraine shall adhere to the Treaty on the Nonproliferation of Nuclear Weapons of July 1, 1968 as non-nuclear weapon states Parties in the shortest possible time, and shall begin immediately to take all necessary action to this end in accordance with their constitutional practices.

ARTICLE VI

1. Each Party shall ratify the Treaty together with this Protocol in accordance with its own constitutional procedures. The Republic of Byelarus, the Republic of Kazakhstan, the Russian Federation, and Ukraine shall exchange instruments of ratification with the United States of America. The Treaty shall enter into force on the date of the final exchange of instruments of ratification.

2. This Protocol shall be an integral part of the Treaty and shall remain in force throughout the duration of the Treaty. Done at Lisbon on May 23, 1992, in five copies, each in the Byelarusian, English, Kazakh, Russian, and Ukrainian languages, all texts being equally authentic.

For the Republic of Byelarus:	P. Kravchanka
For the Republic of Kazakhstan:	T. Zhukeyev
For the Russian Federation:	A. Kozyrev
For Ukraine:	A. Zlenko
For the United States of America:	James A. Baker, III

United States Information Agency

NEWS RELEASE

December 13, 1993

U.S., Kazakhstan Sign Nuclear Dismantlement Pact

By Jim Shevis
USIA Correspondent

ALMATY, Kazakhstan – Vice President Al Gore and Kazakhstan's President Nursultan Nazarbayev signed an agreement December 13 that provides for United States assistance in the ultimate destruction of Kazakhstan's nuclear weapons arsenal.

At a joint press conference following the signing ceremony, Gore told reporters the Safe, Secure Dismantlement (SSD) agreement – together with other pacts signed during his brief visit here – "mark the beginning of an entirely new relationship between Kazakhstan and the United States."

Kazakhstan, the second largest of the former Soviet republics, inherited its nuclear weapons when it declared its national independence nearly three years ago, December 16, 1991. Russia, Ukraine and Belarus also have such weapons.

The SSD agreement provides the legal framework for a series of implementing measures for the safe, secure transportation, storage and destruction of nuclear and other weapons of mass destruction, and to guard against their proliferation.

The U.S. Congress has authorized up to $1,200 million to assist the New Independent States (NIS) of the former Soviet Union for such purposes. Kazakhstan has been allocated $84 million to carry out the implementing measures.

The bulk of initial U.S. assistance – $70 million – will go toward helping Kazakhstan meet its destruction obligations

110

under the START I treaty – for example, destroying underground missile silos.

Susan Koch, special assistant to the assistant secretary of defense for nuclear security and counterproliferation, signed the five implementing agreements, together with General Alibek Kasymov, chief of staff of Kazakhstan's armed forces.

Signing of the SSD agreement capped Gore's short stay in Kazakhstan, the first visit by an American vice president to this Central Asian country.

Perhaps equally as important as the SSD signing was Nazarbayev's announcement that Kazakhstan's parliament had ratified the Nuclear Nonproliferation Treaty (NPT) just hours before the SSD signing.

The goals of the NPT are to prevent further spread of nuclear weapons, foster peaceful nuclear cooperation under safeguards, and encourage negotiations to end the nuclear arms race with a view to general and complete disarmament.

Ratification of the NPT is a "historic decision on the part of your parliament," Gore told Nazarbayev. One hundred-sixty other nations already are parties to the treaty.

Strobe Talbott, ambassador-at-large and special assistant to Secretary of State Warren Christopher on the NIS, later told reporters that there was some resistance to the NPT decision by old-time hard-liners. But in the end the measure passed easily.

"I was told there were 255 deputies present, and it was almost unanimous," he said...

Los Angeles Times

February 15, 1994

U.S. Pledges $400 Million to Kazakhs

Aid: Announcement comes during visit by president of former Soviet republic. In return, it will destroy nuclear arsenal.

By John M. Broder
Times Staff Writer

WASHINGTON—President Clinton pledged nearly $400 million in aid to oil-rich Kazakhstan on Monday after the former Soviet republic agreed to adhere to the Nuclear Nonproliferation Treaty and destroy its nuclear weapons.

Clinton announced the economic assistance in a White House ceremony with Kazakh President Nursultan Nazarbayev, who presented Clinton with documents formally acceding to the nonproliferation pact.

The large increase in aid to Kazakhstan which last year received $91 million from Washington was conditional upon the country's willingness to dismantle more than 1,00 nuclear warheads left over from the Soviet arsenal and to adopt Western-style economic reforms. Nazarbayev has been courting Western investment and technical assistance, particularly in his country's energy and mining industries.

Clinton also said that Kazakhstan is taking the first steps toward affiliation with the North Atlantic Treaty Organization and that the United States and Kazakhstan may conduct joint military training as early as this year.

The moves represent progress toward the Administration's goals of reducing the threat of nuclear proliferation and fostering free-market economic reforms in the states of the former Soviet Union...

Clinton said that Nazarbayev's leadership in nuclear issues and in pushing the Central Asian republic toward democracy and open markets "will also allow Kazakhstan and the United States to develop a full and mutually beneficial partnership."

In addition to the $170 million for nuclear dismantlement, the United States will provide $226 million to help Kazakhstan improve telecommunications, build a stronger banking industry, convert its defense plants to civilian use and develop its abundant natural resources...

Said Clinton: "The United States looks forward to being Kazakhstan's friend and partner in the months and the years ahead. We believe we have established the basis for a long-term partnership of immense strategic importance and economic potential for the United States."

THE WHITE HOUSE

WASHINGTON

November 25, 1994

President Nursultan Abishevich Nazarbayev
Almaty, Republic of Kazakhstan

Dear Mr. President:

I am writing to congratulate you on the successful conclusion of our joint effort to transfer nuclear materials from Kazakhstan to secure storage in the United States. I applaud the leadership you have shown in this unprecedented nonproliferation initiative. This important operation, carried out by United States and Kazakhstani teams working together, is a milestone in our mutual nonproliferation efforts. It reflects an expansion of trust in the maturing partnership between our two nations.

I know that you are taking measures to ensure the security of all nuclear materials on the territory of your country. I commend your responsible actions in this regard. You deserve the world's praise.

Nonproliferation is a key national security objective for me as I know it is for you. I am very grateful that we are able to work together on this effort. I look forward to seeing you again very soon at the CSCE Summit in Budapest, where I will congratulate you personally for your leadership in bringing the START I Treaty into force. Our Budapest meeting will serve as an effective public demonstration of our mutual commitment to the goals of disarmament and nonproliferation.

Sincerely,

William J. Clinton

SPEECH OF HONORABLE BENJAMIN A. GILMAN
IN THE HOUSE OF REPRESENTATIVES
TUESDAY, NOVEMBER 29, 1994

- Mr. GILMAN. Mr. Speaker, I want to take a moment to commend our Departments of State, Defense, and Energy for their recent, successful effort to remove about 600 kilograms of highly enriched uranium from the newly independent state of Kazakhstan.

- The Government of Kazakhstan also deserves our strong commendation for the very constructive role it has played in Operation Sapphire. As we all know by now, the American and Kazakh Governments have worked closely over the past few months to secure the weapons grade material and then transport it safely to the United States, where it is now secure from possible theft.

- Mr. Speaker, before Operation Sapphire began, Kazakhstan had already agreed to also relinquish the powerful nuclear weapons that it had inherited from the former Soviet Union. Frankly, given Kazakhstan's actions in this regard and in carrying out Operation Sapphire, it strikes me that that country is proving itself to be a responsible member of the international community, deserving of the assistance we are now providing to help it implement economic and political reforms.

- Mr. Speaker, I hope that all of my colleagues will join me in commending those of our American agencies that planned and carried out Operation Sapphire, and in commending the Government of Kazakhstan for its very responsible actions in this matter. Together, the United States and Kazakhstan have prevented 20 or more nuclear weapons from falling into the hands of terrorists.

The most extraordinary thing about Project Sapphire was not the secrecy, nor was it how smoothly the planning and implementation went, nor was it the cooperation of Kazakhstani officials with the sometimes-fractious Washington bureaucracy.

What was truly extraordinary, and what was an enormous credit to the Nunn-Lugar program, was the fact that when President Nursultan Nazarbayev—Kazakhstan's former Communist party boss and its first president after the Soviet Union disintegrated—discovered that there was a huge quantity of bomb-grade highly enriched uranium on the territory of his new central Asian state, he called the president of the United States half a world away and asked to have it taken away to safekeeping.

That request was historic, but it was no accident of history: Nazarbayev's call was a testament to his commitment to associate his new country with the West and his trust in the sincerity of American goodwill and cooperation. That trust, and the phone call that launched Project Sapphire, had been earned by the United States through its exercise of Preventive Defense under the Nunn-Lugar program...

DOD's Nunn-Lugar program was Preventive Defense at its best, and Project Sapphire was the Nunn-Lugar program at its best. What might have been history's biggest and most devastating case of 'loose nukes' was averted.

Excerpt from *Preventive Defense:*
A New Security Strategy for America,
a 1999 book by Ashton B. Carter and
William J. Perry, Assistant Secretary of
Defense and Secretary of Defense at the
time Project Sapphire was carried out.

The Washington Post

December 3, 1994

Kazakhstan's Uranium

Ever since the Soviet Union collapsed three years ago, there has been deep concern about the security of its nuclear armory. When the former Soviet republic of Kazakhstan approached the United States about a large stock of highly enriched uranium it was holding, the Clinton administration responded vigorously and successfully. After months of intricate negotiations with the Russians as well as the Kazakhs, followed by careful technical preparations, the uranium has now been transferred to Oak Ridge, Tennessee.

There is about 600 kilograms of it, enough for a relatively unsophisticated laboratory to produce some two-dozen nuclear bombs. A number of governments with nuclear ambitions, as well as a number of terrorist organizations, are hungry for this uranium. It was the first time that Soviet nuclear material has been brought into this country to keep it off the weapons market. An important precedent has been set—and it is a good one.

There will very probably be other cases like this one, in which the United States has to move decisively to ensure the security of the most dangerous remnants of the Cold War.

The transfer of the Kazakh uranium to safety at Oak Ridge testifies to the skill of the diplomats and technicians who carried it off. But it's also a warning to think carefully about other nuclear caches open to illicit sale or theft.

Memorandum on Security Assurances in Connection with the Republic of Kazakhstan's Accession to the Treaty on the Nonproliferation of Nuclear Weapons

The Republic of Kazakhstan, the Russian Federation, the United Kingdom of Great Britain and Northern Ireland, and the United States of America,

Welcoming the Accession of the Republic of Kazakhstan to the Treaty on the Nonproliferation of Nuclear Weapons as a non-nuclear-weapon state,

Taking into account the commitment of the Republic of Kazakhstan to eliminate all nuclear weapons from its territory within a specified period of time,

Noting the changes in the world-wide security situation, including the end of the Cold War, which have brought about conditions for deep reduction in nuclear forces,

Confirm the following:

1. The Russian Federation, the United Kingdom of Great Britain and Northern Ireland, and the United States of America, reaffirm their commitment to the Republic of Kazakhstan, in accordance with the principles of the CSCE Final Act, to respect the independence and sovereignty and the existing borders of the Republic of Kazakhstan.

2. The Russian Federation, the United Kingdom of Great Britain and Northern Ireland, and the United States of America, reaffirm their obligation to refrain from the threat or use of force against the territorial integrity or political independence of the Republic of Kazakhstan, and that none of their weapons will ever be used against the Republic of Kazakhstan except in self-defense or otherwise in accordance with the Charter of the United Nations.

3. The Russian Federation, the United Kingdom of Great Britain and Northern Ireland, and the United States of America, reaffirm their commitment to the Republic of Kazakhstan, in accordance with the principles of the CSCE Final Act, to refrain from economic coercion designed to

subordinate to their own interest the exercise by the Republic of Kazakhstan of the rights inherent in its sovereignty and thus to secure advantages of any kind.

4. The Russian Federation, the United Kingdom of Great Britain and Northern Ireland, and the United States of America, reaffirm their commitment to seek immediate United Nations Security Council action to provide assistance to the Republic of Kazakhstan, as a non-nuclear-weapon state party to the Treaty on the Nonproliferation of Nuclear Weapons, if the Republic of Kazakhstan should become a victim of an act of aggression or an object of a threat of aggression in which nuclear weapons are used.

5. The Russian Federation, the United Kingdom of Great Britain and Northern Ireland, and the United States of America, reaffirm, in the case of the Republic of Kazakhstan, their commitment not to use nuclear weapons against any non-nuclear-weapon state party to the Treaty on the Nonproliferation of Nuclear Weapons, except in the case of an attack on themselves, their territories or dependent territories, their armed forces, or their allies, by such a state in association or alliance with a nuclear weapon state.

6. The Republic of Kazakhstan, the Russian Federation, the United Kingdom of Great Britain and Northern Ireland, and the United States of America will consult in the event a situation arises which raises a question concerning these commitments.

This Memorandum will become applicable upon signature.

Signed in four copies in the Kazakh, English and Russian languages, the English and Russian texts having equal validity. The Kazakh-language text shall be deemed to be of equal validity when its conformity with the English-language text is established.

For the Republic of Kazakhstan   Nursultan Nazarbayev
For the United States of America   William J. Clinton
For the Russian Federation   Boris Yeltsin
For the United Kingdom of Great Britain and Northern Ireland   John Major

U.S.-Kazakhstan Agreement to Seal Up World's Largest Nuclear Test Tunnel Complex

The Defense Department announced today the signing of a Cooperative Threat Reduction (CTR) agreement with the Republic of Kazakhstan that would permanently close and seal the former Soviet Union's Degelen Mountain nuclear test tunnel complex at the Semipalatinsk site. It is the largest such complex in the world...

The former Soviet Union conducted underground nuclear tests at the Degelen Mountain Complex from 1961 to 1989. The U.S.-Kazakhstan cooperative project will demilitarize the complex using environmentally sound methods to close and seal permanently its tunnels. By foreclosing future use of the complex, this project will have a positive impact on our broader efforts to enhance U.S. national security as well as international security in the post-Cold War era...

The Department of Defense is pleased to be engaged in this highly significant cooperative undertaking with the newly independent Republic of Kazakhstan, and sees it as a symbol of both countries' commitment to leadership in promoting global nonproliferation policies.

Excerpt from the U.S. Department of
Defense news release, October 3, 1995

The two Presidents praised the extensive U.S.-Kazakhstan cooperation on issues related to nonproliferation of nuclear and non-nuclear weapons. During President Nazarbayev's visit to Washington agreements were signed on Peaceful Nuclear Cooperation, Defense Cooperation on Counter-Proliferation, and Long-term Disposition of Aktau BN-350 Nuclear Material, among other agreements.

President Clinton welcomed President Nazarbayev's firm commitment to prevent the transfer of technology and materials associated with weapons of mass destruction, and sophisticated military technologies, to countries that pose a threat to regional and global security. The United States and Kazakhstan agreed to establish a regular experts' dialogue on nonproliferation issues.

> Excerpt from the Joint Statement by
> President William J. Clinton and
> President Nursultan Nazarbayev on
> Kazakhstan-U.S. Relations,
> Washington, DC, November 18, 1997

Kazakhstan's firm choice to be a non-nuclear weapons state and to eliminate weapons of mass destruction infrastructure has set an example for the entire world. The legacy of the tests at Semipalatinsk serves as a tragic reminder of the consequences of nuclear testing and as an incentive to redouble our efforts to ratify the comprehensive test ban treaty. I intend to carry this message to the leaders of South Asia.

> Excerpt from a March 20, 2000, letter by
> President William J. Clinton to
> President Nursultan Nazarbayev as
> President Clinton prepared to leave for a
> visit to India and Pakistan

122

Los Angeles Times

July 30, 2000

KAZAKHSTAN

Last of Once Largest A-Test Site Destroyed

U.S. and Kazakh officials completed destruction of what was once the world's largest atomic test ground. More than 500 nuclear explosions were carried out at the Semipalatinsk complex in northeastern Kazakhstan during the Cold War. But more than a decade after the Cold War ended, Kazakhs living around Semipalatinsk say they are still living with the consequences of the tests, citing illnesses and contamination of the land. "On 29 July we closed the last nuclear weapons test tunnel at Semipalatinsk, using 100 tons of chemical explosives," a U.S. Pentagon official said.

From *Times* Wire Reports

SPEECH OF HONORABLE RICHARD G. LUGAR
IN THE UNITED STATES SENATE
THURSDAY, JULY 26, 2001

Mr. LUGAR. Madam President, earlier this month, the United States and the country of Kazakhstan successfully completed one of the most ambitious nonproliferation projects undertaken in history—the securing of one of the world's largest stockpiles of weapons-grade plutonium under the auspices of the Nunn-Lugar Cooperative Threat Reduction program. The security surrounding some three tons of plutonium—sufficient to make some 400 bombs—was enhanced and, commencing in 1998, the fuel assemblies containing spent nuclear fuel were packaged to prevent theft.

In August of 1998, I visited a torpedo factory in Almaty, then the capital of Kazakhstan, that had been converted to manufacture the big steel canisters in which the plutonium-rich assemblies were packaged and sealed. The last canister was sealed and lowered into a cooling pond in early July of this year.

Last week, *The Washington Times* carried a special report by Christopher Pala on this program under the title of "Kazakh Plutonium Stores Made Safe." I ask unanimous consent that this article be printed in the Record and urge all of my colleagues to inform themselves about a real success story in U.S.-Kazakhstan relations.

The Washington Times

July 21, 2001

Kazakh Plutonium Stores Made Safe

By Christopher Pala
Special to the Washington Times

ALMATY, KAZAKHSTAN—U.S. officials last week voiced quiet satisfaction after one of the world's largest stockpiles of weapons-grade plutonium, located in a sensitive zone, was successfully made theft-proof in what the Energy Department called "one of the world's largest and most successful nonproliferation projects."

More than three tons of plutonium, enough to make about 400 bombs, had been stored in a fast breeder reactor on the Caspian Sea shore in security conditions one early visitor described as similar to those of an office building.

Today, the plutonium has been fully secured, said Trisha Dedik, director of the U.S. Department of Energy's Office of Nonproliferation Policy, in an interview July 13 in Almaty, Kazakhstan's economic capital. "It's been a great success."

...The packing is designed to last 50 years, but the plutonium isn't destined to stay at the closed Aktau plant that long.

Eventually, under a decree signed six months ago by Mr. Nazarbayev, the canisters will be taken 2,750 miles by train to the former nuclear-testing grounds at Semipalatinsk, on the other side of this country four times the size of Texas.

There, silos will be dug into the steppe and the fat cylinders will be buried, using a technique perfected in the United States.

United States Senate

107th Congress
1st Session

SENATE RESOLUTION 194

CONGRATULATING THE PEOPLE AND GOVERNMENT OF KAZAKHSTAN ON THE TENTH ANNIVERSARY OF THE INDEPENDENCE OF THE REPUBLIC OF KAZAKHSTAN

Approved unanimously on December 20, 2001

Whereas, on December 16, 2001, Kazakhstan will celebrate 10 years of independence;

Whereas, since gaining its independence, Kazakhstan has made significant strides in becoming a stable and peaceful nation that provides economic opportunity for its people;

Whereas Kazakhstan continues to face political, ethnic, economic, and environmental challenges;

Whereas Kazakhstan plays an important role in Central Asia by virtue of its large territory, ample natural resources, and strategic location;

Whereas the Department of Energy estimates that Kazakhstan has up to 17,600,000,000 barrels of proven petroleum reserves and up to 83,000,000,000,000 cubic feet of proven natural gas reserves;

Whereas Kazakhstan has successfully partnered with United States companies in the development of its petroleum and natural gas resources;

Whereas in November 2001, the Caspian Pipeline Consortium was inaugurated, providing the first major pipeline to bring the Caspian energy resources to the world market;

Whereas the United States private sector contributed nearly 50 percent of the $2,600,000,000 Caspian Pipeline Consortium investment;

126

Whereas Kazakhstan, under the leadership of President Nursultan Nazarbayev, has fully cooperated with the United States on national security concerns, including combating nuclear proliferation, international crime, and narcotics trafficking;

Whereas, since September 11, 2001, cooperation with Kazakhstan and other Central Asian States, specifically Tajikistan and Uzbekistan, has become even more important to the ability of the United States to protect the United States homeland; and

Whereas Kazakhstan has extended all due cooperation to the United States in fighting a war against international terrorism: Now, therefore, be it

Resolved, That the Senate—
(1) congratulates the people of Kazakhstan and its government, on the tenth anniversary of its independence;
(2) welcomes the partnership between the Government of Kazakhstan and United States companies in developing its natural resources in an environmentally sustainable manner;
(3) applauds the cooperation between the Government of Kazakhstan and the Government of the United States on matters of national security and is grateful for the full cooperation of Kazakhstan in the war against international terrorism;
(4) encourages the Government of Kazakhstan to continue to make progress in the areas of institutionalizing democracy, respecting human rights, reducing corruption, and implementing broad-based market reforms; and
(5) looks forward to further enhancing the economic, political, and national security cooperation between Kazakhstan and the United States.

Joint Statement
by President George W. Bush
and President Nursultan Nazarbayev
on the New Kazakhstan-American Relationship

Washington, DC

December 21, 2001

We declare our commitment to strengthen the long-term, strategic partnership and cooperation between our nations, seeking to advance a shared vision of a peaceful, prosperous and sovereign Kazakhstan in the 21st Century that is increasingly integrated into the global economy and the community of democratic nations. To this end, we will advance our cooperation on counterterrorism and nonproliferation, democratic political and free-market economic reform, and market-based investment and development of energy resources.

These goals further reflect our recognition that the threats of terrorism and proliferation of weapons of mass destruction endanger the security not only of the United States and Kazakhstan, but of the world at large. We therefore seek to develop our security cooperation to address these challenges and foster cooperation among Kazakhstan, its Central Asian neighbors, the United States, and our European friends, partners, and allies. In pursuit of these objectives, we are determined to deepen cooperation bilaterally and within NATO's Partnership for Peace.

We reiterate our intent to cooperate in the war against terrorism to its conclusion and within the framework of the international coalition. We underscore our support for a broad-based Afghan government at peace internally and with its neighbors. We also pledge our readiness to cooperate in Afghanistan's reconstruction.

Recognizing that Kazakhstan was the first country to renounce its nuclear-weapons status voluntarily, we reaffirm

128

our mutual commitment to the nonproliferation of weapons of mass destruction. Both sides agree on the need for urgent attention to improving the physical protection and accounting of all nuclear, chemical, and biological weapons materials in all possessor states, and to preventing illicit trafficking in these materials. We pledge to expand our cooperation on these matters under the United States-Kazakhstan Cooperative Threat Reduction Agreement.

In the spirit of partnership, Kazakhstan and the United States intend to strengthen joint activity in ensuring security and stability in Central Asia. We agree that the expansion of trade and economic ties among the states of Central Asia, and deepening of regional integration in important areas, such as the environment, water resources, and transportation systems are a basis for regional security. The United States will consider enhancing assistance programs to Kazakhstan to strengthen border security and to increase the defensive capabilities of the Armed Forces of the Republic of Kazakhstan.

We recognize that free market economies and the rule of law provide the most effective means to advance the welfare of our citizens and the stability of our societies. The United States and Kazakhstan pledge to advance our bilateral economic, trade, and investment relations, including through expanded contacts between the business communities of our countries. We will strive to further develop an attractive, transparent and predictable investment climate. Achieving this goal requires removal of legislative and administrative barriers to investment, strengthening respect for contracts and the rule of law, reducing corruption, and enhancing Kazakhstan's strong record on economic reform.

We also intend to cooperate to advance Kazakhstan's integration in the global economy by supporting Kazakhstan's accession to the World Trade Organization on the basis of standard and agreed criteria, and its graduation from the Jackson-Vanik Amendment.

We affirm our desire to strengthen our energy partnership to diversify export options for Kazakhstan's oil and gas and to diversify global energy supplies. We share the view that a key element of this effort is development of multiple pipelines that will ensure delivery of Caspian energy to world markets, unfettered by monopolies or constrained by geographic chokepoints. We welcome the recent opening of the Caspian Pipeline Consortium (CPC) Pipeline and underscore our support for development of the Aktau-Baku-Tbilisi-Ceyhan oil export route on commercial terms. We will also work together to protect the rights of foreign investors and to abide by decisions of courts, particularly of international courts of arbitration.

Recognizing that democracy is a cornerstone of long-term stability, we reaffirm our desire to strengthen democratic institutions and processes, such as independent media, local government, pluralism, and free and fair elections. We also reiterate our mutual commitments to advance the rule of law and promote freedom of religion and other universal human rights as promoted by the United Nations and the Organization for Security and Cooperation in Europe, of which we are both members. Finally, we pledge to enhance understanding between the citizens of our two countries by promoting people-to-people exchanges, initiatives of non-governmental organizations, and contacts between business people.

The Washington Times

February 25, 2003

Former Soviet Nation May Be Model for Iraq
Disarmament, tolerance, peacemaking set it apart in Asia

By Christopher Pala
The Washington Times

ALMATY, Kazakhstan—President Nursultan Nazarbayev, who in 1991 inherited from the Soviet Union a trove of weapons of mass destruction, is urging Iraq to follow his nation's example and disarm.

"We gained a lot from giving them up. Iraq should look at us as a model," Mr. Nazarbayev told *The Washington Times* in an interview.

When Kazakhstan became an independent country, public opinion was not in favor of disarmament, he said.

"Most people wanted to keep them," Mr. Nazarbayev, 62, said in his office in Almaty last week. "The general opinion was, what kind of country gives away such powerful weapons? Everyone will respect us if we keep them."

The arsenal included one of the world's largest anthrax production facilities and other biological weapons in the northern town of Stepnogorsk, the world's most sophisticated bioweapons testing ground on an island in the Aral Sea, 1,100 nuclear warheads placed in hundreds of intercontinental ballistic missiles, and the world's largest nuclear testing ground in Semipalatinsk, near the border with China.

131

Mr. Nazarbayev gave the weapons up under international supervision, winning praise from the United States and others.

"The international community knows what real disarmament looks like: We saw it in Kazakhstan," Secretary of State Colin L. Powell said last month at the World Economic Forum in Davos, Switzerland.

Mr. Nazarbayev closed Semipalatinsk nuclear testing ground even before Kazakhstan won formal independence from the then-collapsing Soviet Union.

With subsequent financial and technical support from the West, he either destroyed or sent to Russia all the nuclear weapons. The bioweapons plant was destroyed and the bioweapons testing range in the Aral Sea was simply abandoned to scavengers.

A former metallurgical engineer who comes from a family of shepherds, the Kazakh president has since taken on a peacemaking mission well beyond his initial disarmament.

Last June, after 10 years of lobbying Asian leaders, he was able to gather in Almaty the heads of 16 nations representing half the world's population, including Russia, China, India and Pakistan, as well as representatives of Israel and the Palestinian Authority.

The event marked the founding of the Conference on Interaction and Confidence-Building Measures in Asia (CICA).

This month, he organized a meeting of American Jewish leaders with representatives from six Central Asian governments, including two presidents, and Muslim religious leaders.

For an afternoon, more than 60 American Jewish leaders led by Mortimer Zuckerman, chairman of the Conference of Presidents of Major Jewish Organizations, were able to talk with a group of Central Asian Muslim clerics in a friendly atmosphere.

"This is an unusual gathering that would not have taken place in many places," Mr. Zuckerman said. "What makes it unique is that it is sponsored by a government."

Mr. Nazarbayev sees his country of some 14 million people, in which Kazakhs are a slight majority over ethnic Russians and other Slavs, as an example of how Muslims, Orthodox Christians, Roman Catholics and Jews can live in harmony.

Authorities do, however, harass Islamic and Christian groups perceived as extremist, according to the U.S. State Department's Bureau of Democracy, Human Rights and Labor.

United States Congress

Parliament of the
Republic of Kazakhstan

STATEMENT OF FRIENDSHIP AND COOPERATION

We, the undersigned members of the U.S. Congress and the Parliament of the Republic of Kazakhstan, pursuant to the goal of strengthening the long-term, strategic partnership and cooperation between the United States and the Republic of Kazakhstan, are pleased to announce the creation of the U.S. - Kazakhstan Inter-Parliamentary Friendship Group.

Members of the U.S. Congress are encouraged by the Republic of Kazakhstan's commitment to disarmament and the dismantling of weapons of mass destruction, continued economic development as a free market-oriented nation and steadfast efforts to fight against international terror. Kazakhstan has promoted ethnic and religious harmony and tolerance amongst its people and has made important contributions toward the enhancement of regional security through the Asian Security Structure - Conference on Interaction and Confidence-Building Measures in Asia. Members of the Parliament of Kazakhstan are encouraged by the friendship of their U.S. counterparts toward Kazakhstan and praise the high level of trust between our nations.

Both Members of the U.S. Congress and the Parliament of Kazakhstan recognize that: democracy is a cornerstone of long-term stability; the threats of terrorism endanger world security; a free-market economy provides the most effective means to advance the welfare of citizens; parliamentary, cultural and educational exchanges will build the relationship between the peoples of our nations; and in the spirit of friendship and partnership we intend to further expand and strengthen U.S.-Kazakhstan relations through a broad spectrum of bilateral cooperation. To achieve these goals, the two groups are committed to working together through various exchanges in the future.

Signed in Washington, DC
May 7, 2003

Robert Wexler (D-FL)
Joseph Pitts (R-PA)
Thomas Petri (R-WI)
Henry Waxman (D-CA)
Joe Barton (R-TX)
Chris Bell (D-TX)
Edolphus Towns (D-NY)
Eliot Engel (D-NY)
Zach Wamp (R-TN)
Darrel Issa (R-CA)
Eni Faleomavaega (D-AS)
Tom Tancredo (R-CO)

Mukhambet Kopei,
   Deputy Speaker of the Majilis
Omirgali Kenzhebek,
   Majilis Member
Ivan Chirkalin,
   Majilis Member
Nurdaulet Sarsenov,
   Majilis Member

Congressional Record

United States of America

Proceedings and debates of the 108th Congress, first session

RECOGNIZING THE REPUBLIC OF KAZAKHSTAN

SPEECH OF HONORABLE JOE BARTON OF TEXAS
IN THE HOUSE OF REPRESENTATIVES
WEDNESDAY, SEPTEMBER 24, 2003

As the center of the former Soviet Union's nuclear and biological weapons programs, Kazakhstan held considerable—and potentially dangerous—power over the world as the Soviet Union broke apart. In fact, Kazakhstan had the fourth largest arsenal of nuclear weapons in the world larger than Britain, France and China combined. Rather than capitulating to countries offering to pay millions of dollars to purchase these weapons, Kazakhstan's leader, Nursultan Nazarbayev, boldly chose instead to destroy the country's stockpile and position Kazakhstan as a stabilizing force in the region. Mr. President, in light of September 11, threats from North Korea, and the war and continuing operations in Iraq, Kazakhstan's courageous decision against becoming a nuclear state certainly has helped the world avoid greater threats to peace and stability.

Kazakhstan has consistently supported the United States in the War on Terror. Kazakhstan granted to the United States overflight rights and access to its airbase at Almaty. Kazakhstan also participates in NATO's International Security Assistance Force in Afghanistan.

Kazakhstan's contributions have not gone unnoticed. During a visit to Kazakhstan in July 2003, the NATO Secretary General praised Kazakhstan for its support of the peace keeping mission in Iraq and its support for the War on Terror. Kazakhstan was the first Central Asian republic to join in the post-war reconstruction efforts. In August 2003, Kazakhstan sent 27 military personnel, including de-mining experts, engineers, and translators to Iraq.

The illustrations of Kazakhstan's tangible efforts to join the democratic world could not be more stark. Kazakhstan chose nonproliferation over possessing nuclear weapons; it chose peace and prosperity over terrorism and strife; it chose a market economy over the communist status quo; and it chose the difficult path of reform over complacency.

The Washington Times

December 18, 2003

Kazakhstan Hailed for Giving Up Nukes

US officials cite it as role model

By Delphine Soulas
The Washington Times

U.S. officials praised Kazakhstan this week for the example it set eight years ago by giving up the world's fourth-largest nuclear arsenal and called for other countries to follow its example.

Sen. Richard G. Lugar and former Sen. Sam Nunn, the champions of U.S. legislation that helped Kazakhstan and other former Soviet republics to give up nuclear materials, were among those at the ceremony marking the Central Asian nation's 12th anniversary of independence on Tuesday.

"Our experience of nonproliferation and disarmament must be ... applied to other countries," said the Kazakh minister of energy and mineral resources, Vladimir Shkolnik, at a symposium co-sponsored by the Nuclear Threat Initiative, a privately financed group aiming to reduce the threat from weapons of mass destruction.

"Iran and other nations could learn from Kazakhstan that a nation can grow, modernize, make progress and gain stature not in spite of renouncing nuclear weapons, but because of it," said Mr. Nunn.

Kazakh Ambassador Kanat Saudabayev pointed out that Kazakhstan was the first country ever to shut down a nuclear-

138

test site and renounce a nuclear arsenal—the world's fourth-largest at the time.

When the Soviet Union collapsed in 1991, Kazakhstan inherited 104 intercontinental ballistic missiles, 1,040 nuclear warheads, 40 strategic bombers and the Semipalatinsk nuclear-test site, where the Soviet Union conducted more than 400 nuclear tests between 1949 and 1989.

Through the $100 million committed to Kazakhstan by the U.S. government's Cooperative Threat Reduction program, all nuclear weapons were removed from Kazakhstan by May 1995. Kazakhstan also destroyed the nuclear-testing infrastructure of Semipalatinsk by July 2000.

Mr. Nunn, Georgia Democrat, and Mr. Lugar, Indiana Republican and chairman of the Senate Foreign Relations Committee, were the primary forces behind the enactment of the Cooperative Threat Reduction program in 1994.

"With help from the Nunn-Lugar program, Kazakhstan has systematically banished the legacy of weapons of mass destruction inherited from the Soviet Union," President Bush said in a statement read at the symposium.

UNITED PRESS INTERNATIONAL

December 17, 2003

Soviet Legacy in Kazakhstan Remembered

By Nathan C. Santamaria

WASHINGTON, Dec. 17 (UPI)—Kazakh and U.S. officials reminisced in Washington about how the former Soviet republic gave up the chance to become the first Muslim state with nuclear weapons.

"It could have been very different – there was no shortage of emissaries saying, 'you will be the first Muslim nation with nuclear weapons,'" said Kanat Saudabayev, the Kazakh Ambassador to Washington.

His comments came at a symposium at the Kazakh Embassy Tuesday, the 12 anniversary of Kazakh independence.

Kazakhstan voluntarily dismantled the fourth-largest nuclear arsenal on the planet after it declared independence from the Soviet Union in 1991. It has shed a full quiver of nuclear ICBM's, bombs, a heavy bomber fleet, thousands of pounds of weapons grade uranium, and plutonium production facilities.

"We have earned the moral right to call on the world to follow our experience," Saudabayev said while reading a letter by Kazakh President Nursultan Nazarbayev.

Grim memories of the Soviet-era weapons programs surfaced at the symposium. The Semipalatinsk nuclear test site in Kazakhstan was the laboratory for more than 456 nuclear explosions from 1949-89.

"Nearly 100 explosions were above ground at Semipalatinsk," said former Sen. Sam Nunn, D-Ga., whose legislation with Sen. Dick Lugar, R-Ind., paved the way for much of the nuclear disarmament. "This generated a release of radiation far more severe than Chernobyl."

Nunn was speaking in his capacity as the chief executive officer of the Nuclear Threat Initiative.

Semipalatinsk is now closed, but an estimated 1.6 million people were exposed to radiation in its 40-year history; 500 of every 1,000 newborns in the area show health defects, and the infant mortality rate is up five times from 1950 levels.

Voice of America

January 1, 2004

Looking Back at Kazakhstan's Historic Decision

By Jeff Lilley

Kazakhstan recently celebrated its twelfth year of independence. One of the most remarkable events in the country's short history was its decision to give up nuclear weapons. Now Kazakhstan is a key partner in efforts to stop the spread of weapons of mass destruction. VOA's Jeff Lilley attended a ceremony in Washington marking Kazakhstan's historic decision.

The former Soviet republic of Kazakhstan stretches from snow-capped mountains bordering China to the flatlands of European Russia. It's the ninth largest country in the world, covering an area the size of Western Europe. Its fifteen million citizens come from over a hundred different nationalities.

But ten years ago Kazakhstan was known for another reason: it was the world's fourth largest nuclear power. And it might have stayed that way if President Nursultan Nazarbayev hadn't made a courageous decision. Kanat Saudabayev is Kazakhstan's ambassador to the United States and a close confidant of President Nazarbayev: "It could have been very different. In the early days of independence, there was no shortage of emissaries asking President Nazarbayev to keep nuclear weapons, saying that you are going to be the first and only Muslim nation with nuclear weapons, and you are going to be respected by the whole world. I must say that a significant portion of Kazakhstan's elite of that time was also in favor of keeping this nuclear arsenal."

But President Nazarbayev knew well the horrors nuclear weapons had brought to his country. As a young man he had lived in an apartment in northern Kazakhstan. Tremors from nearby nuclear tests would rattle the chandelier and make the furniture creak, and his two young daughters would run to him, fearing there had been an earthquake.

Four decades of Soviet nuclear testing exposed more than one million Kazakhs to dangerous doses of radiation, and the zone of environmental contamination now spreads over territory the size of Germany and Italy combined.

That suffering motivated Mr. Nazarbayev to defy Soviet leaders by shutting down the test site in 1991. Nine months later, Kazakhstan agreed to give up its nuclear weapons that were left behind when the Soviet Union collapsed. That was the beginning of a remarkable relationship with the United States, the country at which Kazakhstan's nuclear-tipped missiles were aimed.

Kazakhstan joined the Nuclear Nonproliferation Treaty in 1993. Under an innovative program designed by U.S. Senators Sam Nunn and Richard Lugar, America provided funding and expertise to help Kazakhstan fulfill its obligation as a non-nuclear weapons state. As part of the Cooperative Threat Reduction program for the former Soviet Union, the United States assisted Kazakhstan in eliminating its nuclear weapons arsenal and testing facilities. Instead of abetting the nuclear arms race, Kazakhstan was taking steps to curb it.

"I must say that for Kazakhstan all these systems were unknown notions because in the Soviet Union there was no tradition of adhering to international standards of controls in this area," says Vladimir Shkolnik, Kazakhstan's Minister of Energy and Mineral Resources, speaking through a translator. He who oversaw the destruction of Kazakhstan's weapons of mass destruction. "As we worked together, we realized we were doing the same job that is crucial for both of our countries, and while in the past we tried to develop weapons to keep the peace, we now are striving for the same peace by disarming."

These days, former Senator Sam Nunn is co-chairman of the Nuclear Threat Initiative, a private organization that works to reduce dangers from nuclear, biological, and chemical weapons. He believes Kazakhstan can be an example to governments that think these weapons provide more security. Instead of spending millions of dollars on building them, he says these countries should use their resources to build better lives for their citizens.

"Iran and other nations could learn from Kazakhstan that a nation can grow, modernize, make progress and gain stature not in spite of renouncing nuclear weapons but because of it," says Mr. Nunn. "Increasing global security also has a critical economic dimension. In making the decision to disarm, President Nazarbayev also chose to use his nation's resources to build an economic base that would benefit all the citizens of Kazakhstan."

Since 2000, Kazakhstan's economy has grown an average of ten percent a year, and the country has received billions of dollars in foreign investment. Last August, the International Monetary Fund closed its office in Kazakhstan, citing the country's considerable economic progress and the fact that it repaid its debt to the fund eight years early. Minister Shkolnik says Kazakhstan is reaping dividends from its decision to renounce nuclear weapons: "It may be said God expressed his gratitude to Kazakhstan for disarming by now giving us an opportunity to enjoy economic growth."

Sam Nunn believes there's another, perhaps more urgent lesson in Kazakhstan's decision to renounce nuclear weapons. That's the need for countries to work together to prevent nuclear weapons or nuclear materials from falling into the hands of terrorists. He calls it a race between cooperation and catastrophe. "Terrorists are racing to get their hands on weapons of mass destruction," he says. "We are not yet racing to stop them. A nuclear 9/11 would make the World Trade Center attack look like a warning shot. We are long past the time where we can take satisfaction from taking steps in the right direction. A gazelle running from a cheetah is taking steps in the right direction. If a terrorist nuclear device exploded in Washington, New York, Astana, Moscow, or London, what would we wish we had done to stop it, and why aren't we doing it now?"

Richard Lugar, chairman of the U.S. Senate Foreign Relations Committee, says America's cooperation with Kazakhstan provides a model for combating the threat facing the United States: "We must be prepared to apply strong diplomatic and economic authority and as last resort military force, and yet we should not assume we cannot forge cooperative nonproliferation programs with some critical nations. The experience of the Nunn-Lugar program in Kazakhstan has demonstrated that the threat of weapons of mass destruction can lead to truly extraordinary outcomes based on strong mutual interest."

There has been some progress, such as an agreement in 2002 by the Group of Eight industrialized nations to spend twenty billion dollars over ten years to prevent the spread of weapons of mass destruction around the world. And next year's U.S. budget contains a provision that allows President Bush to use nonproliferation funds for the former Soviet Union to address emergencies anywhere in the world...

President Nazarbayev says Kazakhstan has earned the moral right to call on other nations to follow its example in renouncing nuclear weapons.

APPLAUDING KAZAKHSTAN'S
PRESIDENT NURSULTAN NAZARBAYEV

SPEECH OF HONORABLE GEORGE RADANOVICH
OF CALIFORNIA
IN THE HOUSE OF REPRESENTATIVES
WEDNESDAY, APRIL 27, 2005

Mr. RADANOVICH. Mr. Speaker, I congratulate the President and the people of Kazakhstan on the 10th anniversary of the removal of the last nuclear weapons from their territory within the framework of the Cooperative Threat Reduction program.

I applaud Kazakhstan's President Nursultan Nazarbayev's leadership and courage. Today, we can state with great confidence that the decision of Kazakhstan's leader to renounce the world's fourth largest arsenal of deadly nuclear weapons was made not only in the interest of the mankind, but it has changed the course of world history. As we all know, proliferation of weapons of mass destruction and international terrorism remain major threats to the world in this new century. It is frightful to imagine a scenario where terrorist organizations such as Al Qaeda could have gained access to Kazakhstan's nuclear arsenal.

Mankind is more secure because of the contribution of Kazakhstan and its leader.

Kazakhstan is a universally recognized leader and one of the key players in nonproliferation and deserves praise for its actions. We believe Kazakhstan, under the leadership of President Nazarbayev, will continue to strengthen this role.

Kazakhstan stands firmly by its international commitments in nonproliferation and stands ready to expand this cooperation with the United States. Convincing evidence of the growing cooperation was evident in the signing in the December 2004 amendment to the bilateral agreement on the nonproliferation of weapons of mass destruction which brought the two nations to a new level of cooperation in preventing the threat of bio-terrorism.

Today, we mark not only the successful interaction between our nations in nonproliferation, but also the growing relations of the strategic partnership between the United States and Kazakhstan. Since the first days of independence Kazakhstan has chosen to build a truly democratic and market oriented society, and proved itself as a strong and essential partner and ally of the United States. American people will never forget the support of the President and people of Kazakhstan at the difficult time following 9/11. I would also like to express my gratitude to Kazakh military engineers who have so far destroyed more than 3 million pieces of ordnance in Iraq, and saved the lives of many Iraqis and those of our brave soldiers.

Kazakhstan's continued dynamic development is a pledge of prosperity and stability for all of Central Asia. President Nazarbayev rightfully should get credit for transforming his country into an undeniable leader in political and economic reforms.

Mr. Speaker, again I would like to congratulate the President and the people of Kazakhstan on their achievements and wish this young country full achievement of its potential. With a great deal of optimism, I look forward to the years ahead as the partnership between Kazakhstan and the United States strengthens to benefit the people of both nations and the world at large.

SPEECH OF HONORABLE RICHARD G. LUGAR
OF INDIANA
IN THE UNITED STATES SENATE
MONDAY, APRIL 25, 2005

Mr. LUGAR. Mr. President, today I submit a Senate resolution to celebrate the decision made by Kazakhstan to join the Nuclear Nonproliferation Treaty (NPT) as a non-nuclear weapon state. Ten years ago this month Kazakhstan sent the last Soviet nuclear warhead on its territory to Russia.

With the Review Conference on the NPT in New York starting next week, it is an especially important time to note the progress made toward the NPT's goals, with U.S. assistance, in Kazakhstan.

More than a decade ago, when the Soviet Union collapsed, Kazakhstan became the fourth largest nuclear power in the world. But instead of enlarging the nuclear club, Kazakhstan joined Ukraine and Belarus in turning away from weapons of mass destruction. Courageous leaders chose instead to embrace the NPT in removing all nuclear arms from Kazakhstan.

The world cheered when Kazakhstan formally acceded to the NPT. I am proud of the role the United States played in Kazakhstan's decision and of our role in facilitating the removal of thousands of nuclear warheads and the elimination of hundreds of SS-18 intercontinental ballistic missiles, silos, and command centers. The addition of three more nuclear-armed states would have been a devastating setback for the NPT.

It is particularly important that the Senate draw attention to Kazakhstan's wise and brave choice, as it stands in stark contrast to events in India, Pakistan, North Korea, and Iran. In 1998, the world was shocked by the testing of nuclear weapons in India and Pakistan. In January 2003, the durability of the NPT was shaken by North Korea's purported withdrawal. We have watched for the past two years as the IAEA deliberated over Iran's numerous safeguards violations amid Tehran's threats of withdrawal from the NPT should the body seek to enforce the treaty's provisions.

With these events in mind, we should remember Kazakhstan. Instead of violating international norms and retaining nuclear weapons, Kazakh leaders made the right choice. When searching for success stories, the international community can turn to Kazakhstan.

The Nunn-Lugar Program also assisted Kazakhstan in eliminating the former Soviet nuclear weapons testing complex at the Degelen Mountain Test Tunnel Complex and at Balapan. In close cooperation with Kazakh partners, the Nunn-Lugar program systematically dismantled the complex and sealed nearly 200 nuclear test tunnels and shafts. These facilities will never again contribute to the weapons systems that threatened the world during the Cold War.

The United States, Kazakhstan, and the international community still have much work to do and these efforts will require compromise and sacrifice. The last ten years have shown that nothing is impossible. Both sides have set aside past differences to accomplish this cooperation. Let us continue to approach these challenges with creativity, a willingness to cooperate, and a commitment to the NPT.

United States Senate

SENATE RESOLUTION 122

RECOGNIZING THE HISTORIC EFFORTS OF THE REPUBLIC OF KAZAKHSTAN TO REDUCE THE THREAT OF WEAPONS OF MASS DESTRUCTION THROUGH COOPERATION IN THE NUNN-LUGAR/COOPERATIVE THREAT REDUCTION PROGRAM, AND CELEBRATING THE 10TH ANNIVERSARY OF THE REMOVAL OF ALL NUCLEAR WEAPONS FROM THE TERRITORY OF KAZAKHSTAN

Approved unanimously on May 25, 2005

Whereas at the time of the collapse of the Union of Soviet Socialist Republics in December 1991, 1,410 nuclear warheads on heavy intercontinental ballistic missiles, air-launched cruise missiles, and heavy bombers were located within the Republic of Kazakhstan;

Whereas, on July 2, 1992, the parliament of Kazakhstan approved and made Kazakhstan a party to the Treaty on the Reduction and Limitation of Strategic Offensive Arms, with annexes, protocols and memorandum of understanding, signed at Moscow July 31, 1991, and entered into force December 5, 1994 (commonly known as the 'START Treaty');

Whereas, on February 14, 1994, Kazakhstan formally acceded to the Treaty on the Nonproliferation of Nuclear Weapons, done at Washington, London, and Moscow July 1, 1968, and entered into force March 5, 1970 (commonly known as the 'Nuclear Nonproliferation Treaty');

Whereas, on December 13, 1993, the Government of Kazakhstan signed the Safe and Secure Dismantlement Act (SSD) and its 5 implementing agreements with the United States, and became eligible to receive $85,000,000 in assistance under the Nunn-Lugar/Cooperative Threat Reduction Program;

Whereas the decision of the people and the Government of Kazakhstan to transfer all nuclear weapons from the territory of Kazakhstan to the control of the Russian Federation allowed Kazakhstan to become a non-nuclear-weapon State Party to the Nuclear Nonproliferation Treaty;

Whereas the continuing efforts of the Government of Kazakhstan to pursue cooperative efforts with the United States and other countries to secure, eliminate, destroy, or interdict weapons and materials of mass destruction and their means of delivery provides a model for such efforts; and

Whereas, in April 1995, the Government of Kazakhstan formally transferred the last nuclear warhead from the territory of Kazakhstan to the territory of the Russian Federation: Now, therefore be it

Resolved, That the Senate commends, on the occasion of the 10th anniversary of the removal of the last nuclear warhead from the territory of Kazakhstan, the people and the Government of the Republic of Kazakhstan for their historic decision to rid Kazakhstan of nuclear weapons.

Congress of the United States
House of Representatives
Washington, D.C. 20515

May 22, 2005

His Excellency Nursultan Nazarbayev
President
Republic of Kazakhstan
Astana, Kazakhstan

Dear President Nazarbayev:

We congratulate you and the people of Kazakhstan with the 10th anniversary of Kazakhstan's nuclear free status.

The U.S. Congress is well aware of your personal contribution to global peace and security. The people of Kazakhstan by electing you as their leader have entrusted you with a great responsibility. By closing down the nuclear test site and renouncing the world's fourth largest nuclear arsenal you have shown tremendous courage, and demonstrated to the world at large your firm commitment to make our planet a safe place to live.

You made this historic decision at a difficult time for your country and we know not everyone supported your choice. Today the people of Kazakhstan and the entire world view this step as a tremendous contribution to global security and non-proliferation of weapons of mass destruction. We applaud you and the people of Kazakhstan for choosing not to gain false respect in the world by keeping those deadly nuclear weapons. Instead, you demonstrated courage and foresight by choosing peace and a secure future.

Mr. President, by your actions you have set an example for other world leaders to follow and we are confident that mankind will appreciate your contribution. We also would like to congratulate you on the remarkable political, social and economic achievements of your country. You have managed to accomplish something the leaders of many emerging countries can only dream of. In a very short period of time Kazakhstan has become a respected member of the community of nations. Kazakhstan is now one of the most dynamically developing countries with a growing economy and an emerging democracy.

We are grateful for your contribution in strengthening and broadening relations through the strategic partnership between our nations. Kazakhstan has proven itself as a true friend and reliable partner of the United States and your country's participation in bringing peace and democracy to Iraq is evidence of that partnership. We highly treasure your friendship.

Mr. President, again please accept our congratulations on the achievements of your country and our assurances of support for further development of Kazakhstan as a truly democratic and economically strong nation.

Sincerely,

Edolphus Towns (D-NY)
Eni F.H. Faleomavaega (D-AS)
Eddie Bernice Johnson (D-TX)
Shelley Berkley (D-NV)
James Clyburn (D-SC)
George K. Butterfield (D-NC)
Joseph Crowley (D-NY)
Gregory W. Meeks (D-NY)
Nydia M. Velazquez (D-NY)
Silvestre Reyes (D-TX)
Eliot Engel (D-NY)
Gene Green (D-TX)
Emanuel Cleaver II (D-MO)
Al Green (D-TX)
William Clay Jr. (D-MO)
Charles B. Rangel (D-NY)
Randy Kuhl (R-NY)

Pete Sessions (R-TX)
Patrick J. Tiberi (R-OH)
Steve King (R-IA)
Chaka Fattah (D-PA)
Alcee L. Hastings (D-FL)
Sheila Jackson Lee (D-TX)
Vito Fossella (R-NY)
Henry Cuellar (D-TX)
Ed Pastor (D-AZ)
Kendrick B. Meek (D-FL)
Maurice Hinchey (D-NY)
Danny K. Davis (D-IL)
Cynthia McKinney (D-GA)
Darrell Issa (R-CA)
Tom Price (R-GA)
Chris Cannon (R-UT)

Reprinted from

The New York Times

October 9, 2005

Kazakhstan Says End of Bomb-Grade Uranium Is in Sight

By Ethan Wilensky-Lanford

UST-KAMENOGORSK, Kazakhstan, Oct. 8—More than a decade after pledging to give up its nuclear arsenal, Kazakhstan announced Saturday that it was moving closer to a second goal: ridding itself of highly enriched nuclear reactor fuel, which terrorists could use to construct a crude nuclear bomb.

The announcement in this distant industrial outpost on the Kazakh steppe was made as Kazakhstan's national atomic company, Kazatomprom, and the Nuclear Threat Initiative, an American nonprofit organization, neared the completion of blending down roughly 6,600 pounds of highly enriched uranium to a different form that is suitable for civilian use but is not weapons-grade.

President Nursultan Nazarbayev hailed the news at a gathering of nonproliferation officials here, adding in an interview that his nation would convert its remaining nuclear reactor fuel, and perhaps try to convert fuel from other nations as well.

"Now we are capable of converting the highly enriched uranium, or any remains of that uranium, into low-enriched uranium," Mr. Nazarbayev said. "Maybe one day our factory here in Kazakhstan can be a place where highly enriched uranium from other countries can be processed into a low-enriched form."

The announcement underscored the quiet sense of urgency among nonproliferation officials since the terrorist attacks in

154

the United States in 2001. It also demonstrated a continued area of collaboration between the West and a centralized post-Soviet government in a region where relations have been strained by the slow pace of political and economic changes.

Kazakhstan, the only Central Asian nation left with nuclear weapons after the break up of the Soviet Union, inherited 1,410 atomic warheads in 1991, giving it the fourth largest nuclear inventory in the world.

Mr. Nazarbayev, the former Communist official who has led the nation throughout its independence, committed to destroy or return to Russia all of its arsenal, and the country swiftly rid itself of nuclear weapons – a decision that Western officials said influenced similar choices by Ukraine and Belarus. "I know what a powerful influence that was," said former Senator Sam Nunn, of Georgia, who worked extensively on nonproliferation issues in the Senate and is a co-chairman of the Nuclear Threat Initiative.

But in addition to its vast nuclear arsenal, Kazakhstan also inherited five aging nuclear reactors, all of which used highly enriched uranium, posing a threat of a different sort.

According to the International Atomic Energy Agency, the world's central nuclear regulatory body, as little as 60 pounds of highly enriched uranium is sufficient to make a nuclear weapon.

Given the potential dangers, the United States, along with other nations and the International Atomic Energy Agency, has been helping to underwrite the more secure storage and conversion of highly enriched reactor fuel.

The work has been quietly conducted in several nations, including Romania, Bulgaria and Latvia, and has gone forward in nations that have had strained relations with the United States. For example, the United States National Nuclear Security Administration, the semiautonomous agency in the Department of Energy that works on nonproliferation projects, removed highly enriched fuel from reactors in Libya and Uzbekistan in 2004.

The United States has also encouraged the closure of nuclear reactors that use the highly enriched fuel, or their conversion to use the less dangerous low enriched fuel.

The project here is a cooperative undertaking of the Nuclear Threat Initiative, an organization financed principally by Ted Turner that complements the government's work, and Kazatomprom. It began in 2001, when the Nuclear Threat Initiative approached Kazakhstan and offered to help move the fuel from a reactor near the border with Iran and to the site here, and convert it to low enriched uranium, Mr. Nunn said.

A vice president for the group, Laura Holgate, said it proposed the project because the fresh fuel from Aktau was "falling through the cracks" of programs run by the United States. Kazatomprom and the Nuclear Threat Initiative split the $2 million cost, which included upgrading the plant where fuel is converted. Once the conversion is completed, the fuel will be sold for use in civilian electricity production.

Although Kazakhstan has only a fraction of its former material that could be used for a weapons, nonproliferation experts said its work was not completed. There remains an undisclosed quantity of highly enriched uranium at one other Kazakh research reactor. Mr. Nazarbayev also vowed to convert this fuel.

"If in that reactor there is some highly enriched uranium which can be converted," he said, "we will make sure it will be converted."

The Albuquerque Journal

October 23, 2005

De-Nuking in Kazakhstan

By Michael Coleman
Journal Washington Bureau

UST-KAMENOGORSK, Kazakhstan—Plenty of people know Los Alamos and Sandia National Laboratories once built bombs capable of blowing up the world. Fewer folks realize the labs work hard to make sure that doesn't happen.

This year alone, Congress gave the Department of Energy, which oversees the labs, $1.4 billion to help secure nuclear weapons and materials around the globe.

Earlier this month, after writing about these DOE budgets for years, I actually got to go to Kazakhstan and see the fruits of some of that nonproliferation work.

Kazakhstan is a former Central Asian Soviet Republic wedged between China and Russia. The nation is big- four times the size of Texas and the ninth largest country in the world. A fledgling democracy with an exploding economy, Kazakhstan owns massive oil and gas deposits, which it is smartly leveraging to gain prestige in international affairs.

It also owns a devastating legacy of nuclear destruction. Former Soviet leaders used Kazakhstan's arid steppes and deserts for hundreds of nuclear tests during the Cold War. Today, the painful legacy of those tests haunts the country in the form of mysterious illnesses among people living near the sites, and large swaths of land generally unfit for anything productive.

When the Soviet Union collapsed, Kazakhstan suddenly found itself as the new owner of 1,410 nuclear warheads.

Leaders in some countries, such as Pakistan and Iran, might have had a big celebration and rattled some sabers.

But Kazakhstan decided to go the other way. The Muslim majority country not only gave up its stockpile, but asked the United States for help in getting rid of it.

This is where New Mexico's labs, Sen. Pete Domenici and media mogul Ted Turner come in.

Domenici, chairman of the Senate Energy and Natural Resources Committee, is responsible for securing money for nonproliferation work from Congress and the White House. And he's pretty good at it. At a time when federal programs are suffering tiny budget increases or even cuts, DOE nonproliferation programs got a whopping 11 percent increase this year, according to the DOE.

Once that money is approved, Los Alamos and Sandia scientists get on airplanes and travel to places like Kazakhstan where they consult with scientists on the down-blending and transfer of weapons-grade uranium and plutonium.

In Kazakhstan, the government is busily reprocessing weapons-grade uranium into low-enriched fuel suitable only for nuclear power plants. When I visited, the country celebrated the near-completed task of converting three tons of weapon-grade uranium, enough for several nukes, to low-grade stuff.

I was shocked at the access the Kazakh government gave journalists at the Ulba Metallurgical Plant, a former top-secret Soviet weapons facility where the nuke dismantling is taking place.

I've been to Los Alamos and Sandia and pictures are generally a big no-no without all kinds of approvals. We had no photo restrictions at all at Ulba, which is either a pretty cool policy or kind of scary, depending on how you look at it.

Back to the Kazakh-New Mexico connection. Ted Turner, who owns the 95,000-acre Vermejo ranch in New Mexico and who told me he spends "as much time as possible" in the state, founded the Nuclear Threat Initiative a few years ago with $250 million of his own money.

The nonprofit scours the globe looking to spend its considerable resources on keeping nuke material out of the hands of al-Qaida and other maniacs bent on mass death and destruction.

Domenici, who sits on the board of NTI, said nuclear nonproliferation is a fairly thankless task. It takes vast amounts of money, and it's difficult to say with any certainty that it's effective.

"If we deliver 38 tons of plutonium I don't feel anything-you don't feel it," Domenici told me after I returned to Washington this week. "But if you are spending all that money and nothing happens (no bombs explode) people say 'Well, what the hell are you spending the money for?'"

Turner, a man who knows a thing or two about spending money, said he can't think of a better place to invest his surplus cash than in nonproliferation. The outspoken and affable part-time New Mexican urges citizens to continually remind Congress that there is no greater priority that preventing a nuclear nightmare on U.S. soil or anywhere else.

"The most important thing people can do is inform themselves on the issue and let their representatives in Congress know they want to see some action," Turner said as we stood outside Ulba in the shadow of the Cold War's legacy.

"If they were doing the job that they should be doing, then NTI wouldn't be needed."

The Washington Diplomat

November 2005

World Shows Appreciation as Kazakhstan Finishes Disposal Project of Soviet-era Nuclear Arsenal

By Michael Coleman

UST-KAMENOGORSK, Kazakhstan—World leaders spend a lot of time talking about the tough task of keeping nuclear weapons out of the hands of terrorists.

It is one thing to talk about it, and quite another to actually do it.

The central Asian nation of Kazakhstan has been quietly disposing of its Soviet-era nuclear arsenal for more than a decade now, and the world is finally starting to take notice, and even show its appreciation.

In October, the former Soviet Republic enjoyed a day in the international spotlight when its president, Nursultan Nazarbayev, commemorated the near completion of a project to reprocess three tons of Kazakh-owned weapons grade uranium into lowgrade fuel for nuclear power. The high-grade material could have been used to construct nearly a dozen crude bombs.

Several notable Americans, including media mogul-turned-philanthropist Ted Turner and former U.S. Sen. Sam Nunn, participated in the ceremony here in Ust-Kamenogorsk.

"It is important that we do everything possible to secure and eliminate bomb-making materials so terrorists cannot use them to build a nuclear weapon," Nazarbayev said at a forum near the Ulba Metallurgical Plant, a former top-secret Soviet weapons facility where the weapons are being dismantled and the uranium reprocessed for power plants.

"Kazakhstan was among the first nations in history to voluntarily disarm its nuclear arsenal," Nazarbayev added. "We are calling on all nations to follow our example."

The nonproliferation event in this small Kazakh town just east of the Chinese border aimed to shine a spotlight on the former communist nation's commitment to ridding itself of nuclear weapons. Organizers also hoped to send other countries a message that nuclear weapons are not the surest way to international respect.

Nunn, co-founder of the Nuclear Threat Initiative (NTI) with Turner, said he deeply admired Kazakhstan's willingness to let the U.S. government help secure its stockpile by downgrading the nuclear component. NTI is a U.S. nonprofit agency that works to secure nuclear, chemical and biological stockpiles.

"This is an example of the biblical admonition to convert swords into plowshares," Nunn said of Kazakhstan's nuclear conversion during in an interview with The Washington Diplomat just after he finished touring the Ulba plant with other public officials and journalists.

Kazakhstan's nuclear legacy is significant. It was a major production and test site for the Soviet government, and parts of this sprawling country remain deeply scarred by the damage. People living near test sites continue to complain of strange illnesses, and some still don't trust the water or the land in some parts of the country.

But now the country is trying to chart a different course. In a brief interview with *The Washington Diplomat* and *New York Times,* Nazarbayev said Kazakhstan will continue to convert its high-grade uranium until it is all gone. After that, the Kazakhs might be willing to convert the fuel for other nuclear nations, as well.

"Maybe one day our factory here in Kazakhstan can be a place where highly enriched uranium from other countries can be processed into a low-enriched form," the president said, as bodyguards and a translator stood nearby.

Nunn also said Kazakhstan should be given more credit on the international stage for making this difficult decision in 1991, especially when Kazakh neighbors such as Iran, Pakistan and India remain intent on realizing their own nuclear ambitions. Meanwhile, Kazakhstan's decision to secure and relinquish its nuclear arsenal is widely believed to have influenced similar decisions by Belarus and Ukraine.

"Kazakhstan's diplomacy could be brought to bear in places like North Korea and Iran," Nunn said. "I don't think Kazakhstan's leadership has been given enough recognition by our country and the G8, nor do I think we've used the power of their example nearly to the degree we could."

At the end of the Cold War, Kazakhstan inherited 1,410 nuclear warheads, making it the only Central Asian state with nukes in its arsenal. Among Kazakh people, the inheritance was either a blessing or curse depending on whom you asked.

Today, the president and other government officials staunchly defend their decision to exorcise the nation's nuclear demons. In part because of a seemingly warm friendship with an appreciative U.S. government, Kazakhstan is enjoying 10 percent annual economic growth and increasing influence in world affairs.

Kazakhstan's leaders decided their highly coveted weapons would only create headaches in the form of superpower scrutiny and economic barriers. So the nation sealed a deal with the United States to provide for the nukes' safe disposal.

In an interview with *The Washington Diplomat*, Kassymzhomart Tokayev, the nation's foreign minister, said he had no regrets about his country's choice.

"It was a wise decision, and Kazakhstan has shown itself to be responsible in terms of its international obligations," Tokayev said. "But there are people in Kazakhstan who voice their doubts because they see double standards in the world."

Turner, a founder of the international cable news powerhouse CNN, has put his considerable money and influence to work at NTI. In an interview with *The Diplomat,* Turner urged rank-and-file Americans to prod their congressmen to stay focused on nonproliferation.

"The most important thing people can do is inform themselves on the issue and let their representatives in Congress know they want to see some action," Turner said. "If they were doing the job that they should be doing, then NTI wouldn't be needed."

Nunn, co-author of the landmark Nunn-Lugar Nonproliferation Act during his time as a U.S. senator, agreed that people need to keep the pressure on Congress to pay for securing nuclear weapons around the globe.

"It's a constant re-education process," Nunn said. "People in Congress change, the political atmosphere changes, and an awful lot of people simply don't make it a priority."

The Washington Times

April 28, 2006

A Burgeoning Friendship
U.S.-Kazakhstan Relationship Strengthens

By Kanat Saudabayev

The visit by Vice President Cheney to Astana in early May is a landmark event showing the special priority Washington places on relations with Kazakhstan, a key country in Central Asia. Announcing the visit, the White House said President Bush "asked the Vice President to visit Kazakhstan to meet with President [Nursultan] Nazarbayev to strengthen our bilateral relationship on the basis of our shared strategic interests and desire to promote democratic reform and economic development."

So, why is Kazakhstan important for the United States, and what sort of place is Central Asia? One view sees this region mainly as a potent mix of instability, unsustainable development, rising Islamic fundamentalism, huge energy reserves and great-power competition. Noting such realities, Zbigniew Brzezinski, writing in 1997, included Central Asia in his "arc of crisis." Much has happened since this term was coined. Given today's realities, Secretary of State Condoleezza Rice recently referred to that region as an "arc of opportunity." And if this is true of Central Asia as a whole, it applies especially to Kazakhstan, the most developed and stable country in the region, and at the same time the one moving most effectively towards democracy.

Kazakhstan is important in a number of crucial areas of concern to the United States: the war on terrorism, nuclear disarmament and new energy resources that can help stabilize world markets. On top of that, Kazakhstan's successful experience in building a secular democracy with a market-based economy in a predominantly Muslim society is particularly important as an alternative model for other Muslim states to follow.

Soviet rule left Kazakhstan a heavily armed nuclear power. But independent Kazakhstan chose to voluntarily give up its might, ridding its soil of the world's fourth-largest nuclear arsenal. Far from undermining our security, this bold and wise decision by Mr. Nazarbayev actually strengthened Kazakhstan. Today, when the world is struggling to contain nuclear proliferation, Kazakhstan's example warrants close study and emulation.

Immediately after September 11 Kazakhstan offered the United States support in the war on terrorism. Together with the United States, today we continue working hard to restore normal life to Afghanistan. At the same time, Kazakhstan is one of the very few Muslim majority countries to send troops to Iraq, and the only Central Asian country to do so. We remain committed to our obligations there.

Kazakhstan's large oil and gas reserves, estimated at 100 billion barrels and 200 trillion cubic feet, are too large to ignore in the effort to meet rising global demand. To attract needed investment, Kazakhstan modernized its laws, courts and administration. Nowadays, major companies from the U.S., Europe, China and Russia are Kazakhstan's partners in developing oil fields and export pipelines. Within the decade Kazakhstan will become one of the ten top 10 oil exporters globally. The country also has rich reserves of uranium, which gain strategic importance as the United States and the world again turn their attention to nuclear energy.

After 14 years of reforms, Kazakhstan has moved from an impoverished command economy to a more open, market-based system. Its economy is now larger than all other countries of Central Asia and the South Caucasus combined, and Kazakhs' living standards are much higher than the regional average. This is supported by our people's strong intellectual potential, with more than 200 universities and research institutes for the population of 15 million. Moreover, thousands of bright students are sent to study at high-quality universities on government-sponsored scholarships. That's why the World Bank now confidently lists Kazakhstan as a middle-class country. In a recent letter to the Kazakh leader, President Bush wrote: "The stability and prosperity that your country enjoys stand as a model for other countries in the region."

Even though Kazakhs had no sustained prior experience with open and fair elections, democracy has taken root among them. International observers agree that each recent election has shown steady improvement of its predecessor. This reflects Kazakhs' own growing commitment to their new democratic institutions. In recent competitive elections Mr. Nazarbayev won a decisive mandate to pursue his strategy of persistent, evolutionary development for our country. Against this background, Miss Rice did not exaggerate when she declared in Astana that "Kazakhstan is poised and ready to break a path for a new Silk Road, a great corridor of reform... Kazakhstan's greatest days lie ahead of it. And the United States wants to be your partner."

Notwithstanding some improvements, the region of which Kazakhstan is a part is a work in progress. Central Asia is still plagued by drug and human trafficking, poverty and, in some areas, Islamic fundamentalism. Human-rights violations and corruption persist. Both the causes and impact of these problems extend far beyond our region. The United States cannot flee from the challenges posed by these conditions, and these challenges cannot be met without committed and competent regional partners.

Kazakhstan and the United States share the desire to transform our region, including Afghanistan, into a Greater Central Asia, a region of peace, stability and prosperity. Kazakhstan is the logical and solid lynchpin for this effort and is eager to expand cooperation with the United States and with all others who share this goal.

The upcoming talks between Mr. Nazarbayev and Mr. Cheney provide a timely opportunity for Astana and Washington to coordinate their positions on a wide range of issues. We hope this meeting will give a new boost to strengthening our countries' strategic partnership.

STATEMENT BY THE PARTICIPANTS OF THE INTERNATIONAL SYMPOSIUM, *NUCLEAR WEAPONS TESTING IN NEVADA AND SEMIPALATINSK: SHARED LEGACY, SHARED LESSONS*

Las Vegas, Nevada

June 1, 2006

On the occasion of the symposium, *Nuclear Weapons Testing in Nevada and Semipalatinsk: Shared Legacy, Shared Lessons,* we, the undersigned, express our concern over the continuous proliferation of nuclear weapons in the world, and therefore declare the following.

In the second part of the 20th Century, during the Cold War, the lands of Nevada and Kazakhstan became sites for nuclear weapons testing by the United States and the Soviet Union, and many of our citizens became victims of the radioactive fallout and other contaminants that resulted from the testing. These people tragically came to know the destructive force of weapons of mass destruction. As a result of 928 nuclear tests at the Nevada Test Site, along with more tests at other U.S. proving grounds, and 456 nuclear tests at the Semipalatinsk Test Site, many thousands of innocent Americans and Kazakhs suffered. Many continue to this day to suffer the consequences of nuclear testing.

In 1991, the people of Kazakhstan under the leadership of President Nursultan Nazarbayev permanently shut down the Semipalatinsk nuclear test site and took the courageous decision to voluntarily renounce the world's fourth largest nuclear arsenal.

Kazakhstan has so far remained the only country to make such a decisive and wise move which showed the way to a safer world.

The United States, at the direction of both Democratic and Republican presidents, has maintained a moratorium on nuclear testing, has reduced its nuclear arsenal, and has aided in decommissioning nuclear weapons abroad.

Unfortunately, the age of nuclear weapons development has not ended. To the contrary, the specter of nuclear weapons is spreading.

Today, the aspirations of a number of countries, and of international terrorist organizations, to acquire nuclear weapons are becoming ever more threatening to the future of humankind. Against this background, we are grateful to Kazakhstan for its outstanding contribution to global security. Kazakhstan's leadership and its successful cooperation with the United States to advance the cause of nonproliferation should serve as an example for other countries.

The victims of nuclear testing in Nevada and Semipalatinsk are eternal reminders to the nations of the world to reject developing nuclear weapons, the modern Sword of Damocles that has imperiled humanity for too long, and to join together to rid the world of the threat of nuclear holocaust.

We are most pleased to report that today's Symposium in Las Vegas, Nevada is another step toward further empowering the people of the United States and Kazakhstan to lead all people away from the threat of nuclear weapons, and redress the consequences of earlier nuclear testing. We pledge to work together to strengthen international cooperation to achieve nonproliferation, as we recognize this is the only path we can take to make our planet safe for all nations to pursue a better future for their people.

Shelley Berkley, U.S. Representative (D-NV),
Kanat Saudabayev, Kazakhstan's Ambassador to
the USA, and other symposium participants

Las Vegas Sun

June 2, 2006

Calls for Halting Nuclear Programs

By Launce Rake

Representatives of two countries with long histories of atomic weapons testing programs called for the end of developing new nuclear weapons after a panel discussion Thursday in Las Vegas.

Ambassador Kanat Saudabayev from Central Asia's Kazakhstan told a group at Las Vegas' Atomic Testing Museum that his country, a former republic of the Soviet Union, endured 456 nuclear explosions in the region of Semipalatinsk, which is similar to Nevada's Nuclear Test Site.

Saudabayev joined Rep. Shelley Berkley, D-Nev., and veterans of the American nuclear program in the discussion on the shared legacy of the testing programs.

One difference, Saudabayev noted, was that Semipalatinsk is in a densely populated part of his country. The Nevada Test Site, about 60 miles northwest of Las Vegas, is in mostly unpopulated federally controlled desert.

Both the United States and the Soviet Union stopped nuclear testing in the early 1990s, and Kazakhstan became independent in 1991. While the Nevada Test Site continues to be an active center for national defense work, Kazakhstan has stopped such work at the Semipalatinsk test site. At the time of its independence, the country had the world's fourth-largest nuclear arsenal, but it has since dismantled all of its atomic weapons.

The ambassador, who has represented Kazakhstan since 2000 in Washington, said his country and the United States would continue cooperating to stop nuclear proliferation by countries and terrorist groups.

He did not mention Iran, Kazakhstan's neighbor, however. The Bush administration and allies are concerned that the Islamic republic is on its way to developing its own nuclear weapon, although Iranian officials say they are only pursuing a peaceful nuclear power program. Kazakhstan is also predominantly Muslim.

Following the discussion, Saudabayev, through a translator, carefully phrased his government's position on Iran's nuclear ambitions: "We are concerned in principle with proliferation of nuclear weapons in any country... The issue of Iran needs to be an issue of discussion and negotiation in the international community."

He similarly cautioned against a nuclear weapons development program in the United States. That issue resurfaced recently with the announcement of a planned Defense Department test – now postponed – that would detonate 700 tons of conventional explosives at the Nevada Test Site. Federal officials said the Test Site blast could aid in the development of either a conventional or nuclear weapon.

Berkley said following the panel that the planned detonation, originally scheduled for today but now indefinitely postponed, may not return: "I'm hearing it's dead."

She noted that there were environmental concerns from the state of Nevada and activists around the West. "I'm very pleased the feds have backed off on this," she said. "They could not meet the environmental standards of the state of Nevada. They were not in compliance and could never be in compliance."

Also participating in the panel discussion were seven others, including Mary Dickson, a Salt Lake City resident and activist with Downwinders United, a group that participated in a lawsuit to stop the planned blast at the Test Site. That group believes nuclear testing has exposed millions to sickening radioactive fallout.

"We know what fallout did," she said. "It's impossible to know how many Americans were affected by nuclear testing. Too many people have died and continue to die."

Not everyone on the panel agreed.

Nick Aquilina, a member of the Nevada Test Site Historical Foundation and a former Test Site manager, declined to join the others on the panel in signing a statement condemning nuclear testing and calling for an end to nuclear proliferation.

He told the audience of about 100 people at the session that the work at the Test Site helped build a nuclear deterrence that prevented a third world war.

Other than the bombs dropped on the Japanese cities of Hiroshima and Nagasaki at the end of World War II, he said, "one has not been used in anger since."

Las Vegas City Life

June 8, 2006

Shared Legacy
*Ambassador says Nevada should learn a lesson
from Kazakhstan's nuclear past*

By Matt O'Brien

During his opening remarks on June 1 at the Atomic Testing Museum, Ambassador Kanat Saudabayev shared a story about his homeland Kazakhstan. Saudabayev, through an interpreter, told the gathering of about 80 that the Soviet Union conducted more than 450 nuclear tests in Kazakhstan over a 40-year period beginning in the late 1940s. Finally, he said, the people of Kazakhstan had enough. They pleaded with their president to shut down the Semipalatinsk test site. The president did in 1991.

Saudabayev said the shutdown was comparable to Gov. Kenny Guinn closing the Nevada Test Site.

"I remember well how much pressure the Kremlin put on our president to stand down and not do this step," said Saudabayev in Russian. "But he withstood this pressure and shut down the test site. Moreover, in December 1991, when Kazakhstan finally became fully independent, we decided to voluntarily renounce the world's fourth largest nuclear arsenal, which at the time was larger than the arsenals of France, Great Britain and China combined."

The ambassador, however, was not advocating anarchy in Nevada. He was simply pointing out that even though the Semipalatinsk test site is silent, its effects remain. The environment of the region has been compromised, he said. Cancer and birth defects among residents are common. An estimated

1.6 million people in and around the region have been exposed to radiation.

Saudabayev seemed to say: Learn a lesson from Kazakhstan, Nevada.

"Kazakhstan is a remarkable county that made a difficult decision that has not only paid dividends for its people, but has established a new legacy for them," said U.S. Rep. Shelley Berkley, who hosted the event. "They know through personal experience that the proliferation of nuclear weapons is not in the best interest of humanity. They are leading the way by demonstrating to countries across the planet that if you give up your nuclear weapons, you help create a safer world."

So, Congresswoman Berkley, should we shut down the Nevada Test Site?

"That's interesting," said Berkley. "But we don't want to shut down the Nevada Test Site. We want to use it for appropriate and peaceful means. We have a wonderful resource in the middle of the Nevada desert. However, it should not be abused by the federal government. There should not be nuclear testing there and there should not be conventional testing, either."

Following Saudabayev's opening remarks, a panel discussed nuclear testing and its effects. The panelists included Saudabayev, Berkley, Troy Wade of the Nevada Test Site Historical Foundation, Mary Dickson of Downwinders United and former Nevada Test Site manager Nick Aquilina. The panelists introduced themselves and took questions from the crowd.

The event, Nuclear Weapons Testing – Nevada and Semipalatinsk: Shared Legacy, Shared Lessons, ran from roughly 10 a.m.-12 p.m. It also featured posters and pamphlets that documented the history of nuke testing in Kazakhstan.

"While today's event may not lead to breakthroughs," said Saudabayev, "I strongly believe that our voice will be heard. Our voice is the voice of the people. Many people of the world share our desire for a safer and happier planet. I believe that this event today will help strengthen our joint efforts to promote peace and nonproliferation in Nevada, Kazakhstan and other countries around the world."

174

The Washington Times

June 14, 2006

Embassy Row

Ground Zero

By James Morrison

The ambassador from Kazakhstan, whose country was the first to unilaterally give up its nuclear arsenal, traveled to Nevada, where the U.S. tested atomic bombs for decades, to urge the world to renounce those weapons of mass destruction.

Ambassador Kanat Saudabayev called on delegates at an international symposium in Las Vegas to urge their nations' leaders to follow the example of Kazakh President Nursultan Nazarbayev, who ordered the destruction of more than 1,340 nuclear warheads the country inherited after the breakup of the Soviet Union.

"The world can and should follow Kazakhstan's example and engage in further reduction and elimination of nuclear arsenals and other weapons of mass destruction, prevent their further proliferation, not to mention preventing their acquisition by terrorists," he said, according to a transcript of his remarks released yesterday by the Kazakh Embassy.

"I am deeply convinced our calls for full renunciation of nuclear weapons will be heard in the world because we are talking about values shared by all the people on the planet.

"My country has already contributed to this process and continues along the path. The more countries that follow Kazakhstan's example, the safer and better our world will be."

Mr. Saudabayev said his country paid a heavy price because of the Soviet Union's open-air testing of nuclear weapons at the Semipalatinsk test site in eastern Kazakhstan between 1949 and

1991. Radiation spread over 116,000 square miles, about one-tenth the land mass of the Central Asian nation, and affected more than 1.5 million people.

The United States conducted 928 nuclear tests at the Nevada Test Site, about 65 miles northwest of Las Vegas, from 1951 to 1992, and radioactive elements were detected in cow's milk in Wisconsin about 1,600 miles away.

Rep. Shelley Berkley, the Nevada Democrat who helped organized the symposium, noted Kazakhstan's strategic importance as a future energy source for the United States.

"Kazakhstan is a very important strategic partner for the United States," she said. "The Kazakhstan-United States relationship will continue to grow because of Kazakhstan's strategic location and our need of their oil and gas reserves."

Kazakhstan is bordered by the oil-rich Caspian Sea, Russia and China.

The cooperation begins. President Nursultan Nazarbayev meets President George H.W. Bush and Secretary of State James A. Baker III at the White House in May 1992.

Presidents Nursultan Nazarbayev and George H.W. Bush sign documents on expanding relations between their two nations. The White House, May 19, 1992.

Senators Sam Nunn (D-GA) and Richard Lugar (R-IN) leave the White House after President George H.W. Bush signs the Nunn-Lugar proposal into law, laying the foundation for the Cooperative Threat Reduction Program, December 12, 1991.

Presidents Nursultan Nazarbayev and William J. Clinton initial a series of documents during the Kazakh leader's visit to Washington, DC, in February 1994, opening the way for U.S. assistance in ridding Kazakhstan of its unwanted nuclear weapons legacy.

Five hundred and eighty-one kilograms (1,278 pounds) of weapons grade uranium are loaded on a USAF C-5 aircraft in eastern Kazakhstan to be transported to the U.S. under Project Sapphire. In the wrong hands, the material would have been enough to build at least two dozen nuclear bombs.

President Nursultan Nazarbayev receives Memorandum on Security Assurances from President William J. Clinton as Russia's President Boris Yeltsin looks on at the Conference on Security and Cooperation in Europe summit in Budapest in December 1994.

ҚАЗАҚСТАН РЕСПУБЛИКАСЫНЫҢ ЯДРОЛЫҚ ҚАРУДЫ
ТАРАТПАУ ТУРАЛЫ ШАРТҚА ҚОСЫЛУЫНА БАЙЛАНЫСТЫ
ҚАУІПСІЗДІККЕ СЕНДІРУЛЕР ТУРАЛЫ

МЕМОРАНДУМ

MEMORANDUM ON SECURITY ASSURANCES
IN CONNECTION WITH
REPUBLIC OF KAZAKHSTAN'S ACCESSION TO THE
TREATY ON THE NON-PROLIFERATION
OF NUCLEAR WEAPONS

МЕМОРАНДУМ О ГАРАНТИ
В СВЯЗИ С ПРИСОЕДИНЕНИЕМ
К ДОГОВОРУ О НЕРАСПРОСТРАН

- 4 -

Осы Меморандум қол қойылған сәттен бастап күшіне енеді.
Қазақ, ағылшын және орыс тілдерінде төрт дана болып қол
қойылды, сондай-ақ ағылшын және орыс тілдеріндегі текстердің
күші бірдей. Қазақ тіліндегі текстің ағылшын тіліндегі текс-
ке сәйкестігі қуатталған соң онан да күші бірдей деп санала-
ды.

Қазақстан Республикасы үшін
For Republic of Kazakhstan
За Республику Казахстан

Америка Құрама Штаттары үшін
For United States of America
За Соединенные Штаты Америки

Ресей Федерациясы үшін
For Russian Federation
За Российскую Федерацию

Ұлыбритания мен Солтүстік Ирландия
Құрама Корольдігі үшін
For United Kingdom of Great Britain
and Nothern Ireland
За Соединенное Королевство Великобритании
и Северной Ирландии

Some of the many decommissioned TU-95 bombers.

The remains of one of 148 missile silos destroyed in
Kazakhstan under the Nunn-Lugar Program.

The last test tunnel at the Semipalatinsk test site is destroyed with conventional explosives through joint Kazakhstan-U.S. efforts under the Cooperative Threat Reduction Program in July 2000.

"We know what real disarmament looks like. We saw it in Kazakhstan."

U.S. Secretary of State Colin L. Powell

President Nursultan Nazarbayev meets President George W. Bush in the White House on December 21, 2001. The two leaders declare their commitment to the long-term strategic partnership between Kazakhstan and the United States with cooperation in nonproliferation as a top priority.

U.S. Senator Mary Landrieu (D-LA) presents President Nursultan Nazarbayev with a copy of the Senate Resolution 194, approved unanimously by the Senate on December 20, 2001, as Senator Orrin Hatch (R-UT) and Rep. Joseph Pitts (R-PA) look on, at Blair House, Washington, DC, on the same day.

U.S. Senator Richard G. Lugar (R-IN) (right), co-author of the
Nunn-Lugar Cooperative Threat Reduction Program praises
the way Kazakhstan has worked with the United States on the
program. The cooperation now extends to new areas such as
jointly fighting bio-terrorism. Here, Sen. Lugar visits a biological laboratory in Kazakhstan in a group which included Kanat
Saudabayev, Kazakhstan's Ambassador to the United States
(center). U.S. Defense Department's Andrew Weber shows
them a vial containing the plague pathogen.

Kazakhstan's commitment to global peace and security is demonstrated as Kazakh troops destroy munitions in Iraq as part of the U.S.-led coalition forces. They have already destroyed more than four million pieces of ordnance.

Donald Rumsfeld, U.S. Secretary of Defense on his 2004 visit to Astana meets Kazakh army engineers recently returned from duty in Iraq. He presented the troops with U.S. medals honoring their service.

A growing closeness between Washington and Astana is seen
in a continuing flow of high level visits and meetings between
officials from both countries. Condoleezza Rice, U.S. Secretary
of State, visited Kazakhstan in October 2005, declaring
"Kazakhstan's greatest days lie ahead of it, and the United
States wants to be your partner." Here, she has an animated
discussion with President Nursultan Nazarbayev as
Kassymzhomart Tokaev (right), Kazakhstan's Minister of
Foreign Affairs, and Kanat Saudabayev, Kazakhstan's
Ambassador to the United States, look on.

U.S. Vice President Richard Cheney visited Astana in May 2006. Meeting with President Nazarbayev, the U.S. Vice President said: "We are proud to be your strategic partner."

President Nursultan Nazarbayev participated in the G8 summit in St. Petersburg, Russia, as chairman of the Commonwealth of Independent States. He discussed with other world leaders key issues such as nuclear and energy security.

Presidents Nursultan Nazarbayev and George W. Bush met at the G8 summit seeking to expand cooperation and friendship between their two nations. Kazakhstan supported the Global Initiative to Combat Nuclear Terrorism announced there by the Presidents of Russia and the United States.

The Republic of Kazakhstan

Location:	Central Asia, south of Russia, northwest of China
Total Area:	2,717,300 square kilometers (1,049,149.53 square miles), Ninth largest country in the world
Population:	15,200,000
Statehood:	Regained independence on December 16, 1991
Form of government:	A unitary state with a presidential form of government

Kazakhstan Strongly Condemns Missile Tests by North Korea

Statement by the Ministry of Foreign Affairs of the Republic of Kazakhstan

Astana

July 6, 2006

Kazakhstan strongly condemns the missile tests conducted by the Democratic People's Republic of Korea. Such actions can lead to serious consequences for peace and security in the Asia-Pacific region. We call upon the leadership of the DPRK to stick to the agreements reached within the six party negotiating process. We believe it is possible for it to follow the example of Kazakhstan, which voluntarily renounced nuclear weapons and means of their delivery which became an important guarantee of ensuring security of our country and its successful economic development.

Le Monde

July 13, 2006

My Advice to Iran

By Nursultan Nazarbayev

As the world is concerned with the testing of long range missiles by North Korea and by the intentions of Iran, I would like to share my personal experience. My country, Kazakhstan, since its independence, has opted to become a nuclear weapon free nation and to eliminate nuclear materials which were left on our territory as grim legacy of the past. I believe we have successfully overcome these problems thanks to unwavering striving for peace and stability.

I had to make difficult decisions which were not dictated by political expediency. First of all, they were crucial issues. Our land had seen too many experiments with the "nuclear genie". During 40 years, 456 nuclear explosions were carried out at the Semipalatinsk nuclear test site, including 26 atmospheric, 78 ground, and the rest underground. Almost half a million people were either directly or indirectly affected by consequences of these nuclear weapons tests. Hundreds of thousands of hectares of land are still unusable.

That was why when I became the President of Kazakhstan, I first of all declared a moratorium on nuclear tests. On August 29, 1991, I signed a decree prohibiting any nuclear weapons tests on our territory.

The fate of the Semipalatinsk nuclear test site was not our only worry. In December 1991, when the Soviet superpower collapsed and the Commonwealth of Independent States was born, an issue arose of what to do with the Soviet nuclear arsenal left with the newly independent states. Kazakhstan was left with a huge nuclear arsenal, the world's fourth largest. We had to make a choice based on a civilized approach to this problem. Our country declared its commitment to principles of peace from the very first days of its existence. Only Russia, as a great power, could claim to own and really manage this former nuclear complex.

But the issue of our national security loomed as large for us then as it, perhaps, does now for Iran. At that time, I initiated the process of multilateral and multilayered negotiations which helped us receive security guarantees from major nuclear powers. These powers promised Kazakhstan that if we get attacked they will take immediate measures to rebuke the attack and preserve the territorial integrity of our country, as well as to demand an extraordinary session of the United Nations Security Council.

I must say our status as a nuclear weapons free country has strengthened our positions in the fight for nuclear disarmament, stability, peace in the world and global security. Our renunciation of nuclear weapons has become an important factor of our economic and political development, and our internal stability.

The very existence of weapons of mass destruction, both nuclear, and conventional, cannot be the means to solve problems of global and regional security. I believe the world community is still beholden to its old concepts as far as many issues go. That is why our today's situation is full of paradoxes, ambiguities and half-measures. We need to take into account the fact that the use of nuclear weapons, just as a complete end to wars between countries, is very unlikely; we need to set our sights on the goal of eliminating the threat of terrorism.

Currently, no country of the nuclear club expresses firm desire to renounce its nuclear weapons nor offers to begin negotiations on this issue. It is time to face the reality. It is necessary to minimize the consequences of the expansion of the nuclear club, especially, as far as its illegal and semi-legal members are concerned.

I believe that to ensure global security we must move forward toward full nuclear disarmament, being aware that this type of weapons, like any weapons of mass destruction, is a direct threat to mankind. But here, another problem arises: it is time for all of us to think about using alternative energy resources and about global energy security. There are no reasons to erect obstacles for countries which aspire to have peaceful atom. Iran, like other countries which have or are planning to build atomic power plants, must have the opportunity to conduct scientific and technical research, seek improvements in ensuring safety of its atomic power plants and think about problems with nuclear fuel and waste. This activity must be transparent, and the international community must have the opportunity to supervise it.

I am talking about improving the control over the entire set of problems with nuclear weapons and technology, as well as any activity in the area of peaceful atom, so that there is no use of fissile materials for military purposes. It seems very logical to think of creating an organization under the IAEA's auspices which would ensure the supply of fuel for atomic power plants and manage the storage and processing of waste. This way it will be possible to control any leaks of raw materials needed for the production of military nuclear devices. It is obvious issues of political, commercial and financial nature will have to be resolved to achieve this.

The G8 will have an important role to play, especially in the area of reducing strategic offensive weapons. My proposals may sound unrealistic. But we need to move forward in this direction. The nuclear threat and the proliferation of nuclear weapons have become an inevitable part of the international relations, economy and science. And only by radically changing the situation will we be able to free ourselves of its side products, such as nuclear waste, and to make a step forward to solving global and pressing problems of nuclear security.

Kazakhstan Welcomes Russia-U.S. Initiative Against Nuclear Terrorism

Statement by the Ministry of Foreign Affairs of the Republic of Kazakhstan

Astana

July 15, 2006

The Republic of Kazakhstan welcomes the Global Initiative to Combat Nuclear Terrorism put forward by the presidents of Russia and the United States of America on July 15, 2006, in St. Petersburg.

Kazakhstan condemns terrorism in all its forms and manifestations and believes that terrorist acts with nuclear weapons are among the most acute and dangerous challenges to international security faced by the world community. The threat of such acts today is as real as ever.

The initiative of the Russian Federation and the United States of America will become an important element in strengthening the existing regimes of nonproliferation and is aimed at greater interaction of the world community in preventing components of nuclear weapons from falling into the hands of terrorists," the Foreign Ministry said. "Of particular importance are efforts to ensure safe control over the use, storage and transfer of nuclear materials, physical protection of nuclear facilities, the development of effective means to reduce the danger of consequences of possible terrorist nuclear attacks, the improvement of legal basis for international cooperation and domestic system of prevention of any types of crimes related to movement of nuclear materials.

Kazakhstan, a country which voluntarily renounced its nuclear arsenal views this initiative as a new effective step in the fight against international terrorism. Our support of the Russia-US initiative confirms Kazakhstan's firm commitment to strengthening the international security and to collective efforts of the world community in fighting terrorism.

United States
House of Representatives

109th Congress
2nd Session

HOUSE RESOLUTION 905

CONGRATULATING KAZAKHSTAN ON THE 15TH
ANNIVERSARY OF THE CLOSURE OF THE WORLD'S
SECOND LARGEST NUCLEAR TEST SITE IN THE
SEMIPALATINSK REGION OF KAZAKHSTAN AND FOR
ITS EFFORTS ON THE NONPROLIFERATION OF
WEAPONS OF MASS DESTRUCTION

Approved unanimously on July 18, 2006

Whereas on August 29, 1991, the Government of
Kazakhstan shut down the world's second largest nuclear test
site in the Semipalatinsk region of the Republic of Kazakhstan;

Whereas between 1945 and 1991, more than 450 nuclear
tests were conducted at this site, exposing more than 1.5 million
innocent people to radiation and causing damage to the environment;

Whereas the damage to the environment and to the health
of the people of Kazakhstan from this terrible legacy of hundreds of detonations of Soviet nuclear explosive devices could
be felt for decades to come;

Whereas upon gaining independence, Kazakhstan inherited
from the former Soviet Union more than 1,000 nuclear warheads, as well as a squadron of 40 TU-95 heavy bombers armed
with 370 nuclear warheads, comprising the world's fourth
largest nuclear arsenal;

Whereas Kazakhstan renounced this massive nuclear arsenal, unilaterally disarmed, and joined the Treaty on the
Nonproliferation of Nuclear Weapons (NPT) as a non-nuclear
weapon state, the first time a state that had possessed such a
massive nuclear arsenal had done so;

Whereas Kazakhstan's leadership and cooperation with the United States on nonproliferation matters is a model for other countries to follow;

Whereas Kazakhstan also inherited from the former Soviet Union the world's largest anthrax production and weaponization facility, which had a capacity to produce more than 300 metric tons of anthrax per year;

Whereas Kazakhstan, in cooperation with the United States Cooperative Threat Reduction (CTR) program, dismantled the military-related buildings and equipment associated with the anthrax production and weaponization facility;

Whereas the Government of Kazakhstan, in cooperation with the United States, participated in a very successful secret operation code-named 'Project Sapphire,' in which 581 kilograms (1,278 pounds) of weapons-grade highly enriched uranium, enough to produce 20 to 25 nuclear warheads, were removed overnight from Kazakhstan;

Whereas in December 2004 and May 2006, Kazakhstan and the United States concluded amendments to a bilateral agreement on the nonproliferation of weapons of mass destruction, which have moved the two countries toward a new level of cooperation in preventing the threat of bio-terrorism; and

Whereas in February 2006, Kazakhstan and the Nuclear Threat Initiative of Washington, D.C., with the support of the United States Department of Energy, blended down 2,900 kilograms (6,600 pounds) of weapons-usable highly enriched uranium, enough to produce up to 25 nuclear warheads, converting the material for peaceful use and preventing it from falling into the hands of terrorist organizations and being used in weapons production: Now, therefore, be it

Resolved, That the House of Representatives–
(1) congratulates the people and Government of the Republic of Kazakhstan on the 15th anniversary of the closure of the world's second largest nuclear test site in the Semipalatinsk region of Kazakhstan;

(2) commends Kazakhstan for greatly advancing the cause of the nonproliferation of weapons of mass destruction as a result of its dismantlement of its nuclear and biological weapons and facilities; and

(3) calls upon the Administration to establish a joint working group with the Government of Kazakhstan to assist in assessing the environmental damage and health effects caused by nuclear testing in the Semipalatinsk region by the former Soviet Union.

SPEECH OF HONORABLE ENI F.H. FALEOMAVAEGA
OF AMERICAN SAMOA
IN THE HOUSE OF REPRESENTATIVES
TUESDAY, JULY 18, 2006

Mr. FALEOMAVAEGA. Madam Speaker, I rise in strong support of this resolution. House Resolution 905 congratulates Kazakhstan on the 15th anniversary of the closure of the world's second largest nuclear test site in the Semipalatinsk region of Kazakhstan and for its efforts on the nonproliferation of weapons of mass destruction.

House Resolution 905 is non-controversial and historic. It is historic because this is the first time the U.S. House of Representatives has considered legislation in praise of Kazakhstan, a former Soviet Republic that has proved to be a true ally of the U.S.

It is also historic because it is being considered on the 60th birthday of my friend and brother, His Excellency Kanat Saudabayev, Ambassador of the Republic of Kazakhstan. Ambassador Saudabayev has worked tirelessly to represent the interests of Kazakhstan in the U.S. and has served his President, Nursultan Nazarbayev, with distinction and honor and, today, it is my privilege to wish him a happy birthday and commend him for his service to his nation and ours.

Also, at this time, I thank Chairman Henry Hyde and Ranking Member Tom Lantos of the International Relations Committee for their support in moving this important legislation forward. I also thank Congresswoman Ileana Ros-Lehtinen and Congressman Gary Ackerman, Chair and Ranking Member of the Subcommittee on the Middle East and Central Asia, for cosponsoring this legislation. Without their support, House Resolution 905 would not be possible.

House Resolution 905 recognizes Kazakhstan as a model for advancing the cause of nuclear nonproliferation. After the collapse of the Soviet Union in 1991, Kazakhstan inherited a ruined economy and the world's fourth largest nuclear arsenal. This arsenal could possibly have helped to resolve the financial problems of this young and struggling nation.

However, led by President Nazarbayev, the people of Kazakhstan, knowing firsthand the horrible effects of nuclear tests, made a choice to renounce nuclear weapons. In fact, immediately after achieving independence and in spite of threats from the Kremlin, President Nazarbayev closed and sealed the world's second largest nuclear test site at Semipalatinsk where the Soviet Union conducted more than 450 nuclear tests from 1949 to 1991.

Today, few know about President Nazarbayev's heroic decision which undoubtedly changed the course of modern history. Few know this story because Kazakhstan did not bargain and did not lobby to gain political or economic dividends from its choice. Rather, Kazakhstan, for the sake of global peace and security, consciously chose to ensure a brighter future for their children and ours.

For this reason, I believe we should speak more often of Kazakhstan's example. While I am grateful that the world is aware of the Chernobyl disaster where thousands perished, I am saddened that the world knows so little about the tragedies of Semipalatinsk, the Marshall Islands and French Polynesia where children and the elderly have been dying for decades as a result of Cold War policies that to this day have never been set right.

In Semipalatinsk, the cumulative power of explosions from nuclear tests conducted by the former Soviet Union is believed to be equal to the power of 2,500 explosions of the type of bomb dropped on Hiroshima, Japan in 1945. More than 1.5 million people in Kazakhstan suffered from nuclear contamination as a result of these tests and a horrifying array of disease will continue to destroy the lives of many more.

186

As a Pacific Islander, I have a special affinity for the people of Kazakhstan because the Marshallese and Polynesian Tahitians also know firsthand the horrors of nuclear testing.

In 2003, as a direct result of my friendship with Ambassador Saudabayev, I became aware of the magnitude of the problem of Semipalatinsk. In August 2004, I felt a deep sense of obligation as a Member of Congress who had visited the nuclear test sites in the Marshall Islands and Tahiti to also visit the Semipalatinsk test site. During my visit and in later discussions with President Nazarbayev, I learned that I was the first American legislator to set foot on ground zero in Kazakhstan.

Considering the courageous decision made by President Nazarbayev to shut down the Semipalatinsk test site so that you and I and future generations may live in peace, I believe we have a moral responsibility to bear the burdens of our brothers and sisters in Semipalatinsk. This is why I am pleased that House Resolution 905 calls upon the Administration to establish a joint working group with the Government of Kazakhstan to assist in assessing the environmental damage and health effects caused by nuclear testing in the Semipalatinsk region by the former Soviet Union.

As important as this resolution is, I also believe the international community should more fully acknowledge Kazakhstan's contribution to world peace. While I am pleased that this year's Nobel Peace Prize was awarded to the Director General of the International Atomic Energy Agency (IAEA), I believe President Nazarbayev should also receive the Nobel Peace Prize for reaffirming the worth and advancing the rights of the human person by dismantling the world's 4th largest nuclear arsenal, closing and sealing the Semipalatinsk test site, and most recently blending down 6,600 pounds of weapons-usable highly enriched uranium, or enough to produce up to 25 nuclear warheads, converting the material for peaceful use and thereby preventing it from falling into the hands of terrorist organizations.

I also believe Senator Richard Lugar and former Senator Sam Nunn should likewise be honored for establishing the

187

Nunn-Lugar Cooperative Threat Reduction (CTR) program which provides assistance to Russia and the former Soviet republics for securing and destroying their excess nuclear, biological and chemical weapons.

With the recent announcement of our need to establish a global initiative to combat nuclear terrorism and on the occasion of the 15th anniversary of the closure of the world's second largest nuclear test site at Semipalatinsk, it is only fitting and fair that we should acknowledge Kazakhstan's commitment and leadership in nuclear disarmament and nonproliferation. For this reason, I urge my colleagues to support House Resolution 905 and I thank Minority Leader Pelosi and Majority Leader Boehner for bringing this timely resolution to the floor.

Congressional Record

United States of America

Proceedings and debates of the 109th Congress, second session

SPEECH OF HONORABLE TOM LANTOS
OF CALIFORNIA
IN THE HOUSE OF REPRESENTATIVES
TUESDAY, JULY 18, 2006

Mr. LANTOS. Madam Speaker, I rise in strong support of this resolution. I would first like to commend my good friend and colleague from American Samoa, Eni Faleomavaega, for introducing this important measure. He has been the leader in Congress on matters related to the legacy of nuclear testing, both in the former Soviet Union and in the Pacific, and we greatly appreciate his hard work.

Madam Speaker, upon the dissolution of the Soviet Union, the newly-minted independent nation of Kazakhstan found itself in possession of the fourth largest nuclear arsenal in the world. Kazakhstan inherited more than 1,000 nuclear weapons and a squadron of heavy bombers armed with 370 nuclear warheads from the Soviet Union.

Rather than embrace their nuclear status, the people of Kazakhstan made a farsighted decision fifteen years ago. They closed their nation's nuclear test site, and yielded all of their inherited nuclear arsenal and weapons materials back to Russia.

Kazakhstan, the victim for so long of Soviet domination, completely and voluntarily rescinded their membership in the nuclear club. The nation proudly joined the Treaty on the Nonproliferation of Nuclear Weapons, or NPT, as a non-nuclear weapon state, the first time a state that had possessed such a massive nuclear arsenal had done so.

While Kazakhstan made a wise decision to rid itself of its nuclear arsenal, the damage to the environment and to the health of the people of Kazakhstan will be felt for decades to

189

come. Between 1945 and 1991, more than 450 nuclear tests were conducted at the Semipalatinsk test site, exposing more than 1.5 million innocent people to radiation and causing massive damage to the environment.

It is for that reason that the United States should work with Kazakhstan to establish a joint working group to help assess the environmental damage and health affects caused by the nuclear testing.

Madam Speaker, Kazakhstan's commitment to nuclear non-proliferation, and to nuclear disarmament, is an inspiring one, and a shining example for others to follow. It has strengthened immeasurably the global nuclear nonproliferation regime, and we greatly appreciate these actions.

Madam Speaker, I strongly support this resolution, and I urge all of my colleagues to join me in doing likewise.

Congressional Record

United States of America

Proceedings and debates of the 109th Congress, second session

SPEECH OF HONORABLE ILEANA ROS-LEHTINEN
OF FLORIDA
IN THE HOUSE OF REPRESENTATIVES
TUESDAY, JULY 18, 2006

Ms. ROS-LEHTINEN. Madam Speaker, I rise in support of House Resolution 905, congratulating Kazakhstan on the 15th anniversary of the closure of the world's second largest nuclear test site, and for its efforts on nonproliferation of weapons of mass destruction.

Kazakhstan was once home to the second largest nuclear test site in the world. From the years of 1945 to 1991, over 450 tests were carried out at that site.

After becoming independent from the Soviet Union, Kazakhstan was left with more than 1,000 nuclear warheads and with 40 heavy bombers armed with 370 nuclear warheads and comprising the world's fourth largest nuclear arsenal.

Immediately after achieving its independence, Kazakhstan successfully closed and secured its enormous nuclear test site.

Kazakhstan accepted support from the U.S. Department of Energy and readily complied with the nuclear threat initiative, blending down over 6,000 pounds of weapons grade highly enriched uranium.

Given the threats that we are facing from rogue states such as Iran, which has blatantly violated its nuclear nonproliferation obligations and which refuses to immediately stop its nuclear-related and weapons-related activities, we welcome the opportunity to stand here today commemorating Kazakhstan's landmark decision.

191

In addition to inheriting a massive nuclear arsenal from the Soviet Union, Kazakhstan was also left with the world's largest anthrax production and weaponizing facility.

Through cooperation with the United States Cooperative Threat Reduction program, CTR, Kazakhstan was able to successfully dismantle the military related buildings and equipment related to such anthrax programs.

I ask my colleagues to support this important resolution and, in so doing, join us in commending the people and the government of Kazakhstan on the 15th anniversary of the closure of the world's second largest nuclear test site and for greatly advancing global nonproliferation efforts by dismantling its nuclear and biological weapons and facilities.

SPEECH OF HONORABLE SHELLEY BERKLEY
OF NEVADA
IN THE HOUSE OF REPRESENTATIVES
TUESDAY, JULY 18, 2006

Ms. BERKLEY. Madam Speaker, I rise today to congratulate the people and the Government of the Republic of Kazakhstan on the 15th anniversary of the closure of the former Soviet nuclear test site within their borders. I am pleased to commend Kazakhstan on its tireless work for nonproliferation of weapons of mass destruction, and I call upon the administration and my colleagues here in Congress to assist Kazakhstan in assessing the environmental damage caused by Soviet testing.

This is a very important and very personal issue to me. I represent southern Nevada, where the United States detonated over 900 nuclear bombs at the Nevada test site in the 1950s and 1960s. Nevadans and residents of surrounding States paid a very heavy price for this testing especially during the aboveground testing years. Environmental contamination and the devastating impact on the health of the people living in this area, living in the southwestern region of the United States of America, were unconscionable and unacceptable and can never be allowed to happen again.

I remember as a kid growing up in Las Vegas, so many of my friends' mothers and fathers worked at the Nevada test site. They would be bussed into the test site during the week. They would be bussed home during the weekend. Little did any of us realize that they were being contaminated as they worked for our government in the attempt and in the thought that they were doing something good and important for national security.

I recall, after being elected to Congress, going to a meeting of all the former Nevada test site workers, at least those that were still alive. There were 200 people in the room when I walked in. We asked that everybody in the room that had been a worker at the test site who had some form of cancer, if they would mind standing and acknowledging that fact. Every single person in that room, all 200 of them, stood up because they were all suffering from a form of cancer.

Radioactive contamination from tests in both Nevada and in Kazakhstan indiscriminately spread across the globe, eventually causing world powers to recognize the terrible health risks, stop atmospheric testing, and finally end all testing. We must prevent a return to nuclear testing, and we must continue to redress the problems that have been caused by testing over the last 60 years and continue to cause environmental and health threats from the United States to the former Soviet Union, Kazakhstan, to the South Pacific, Marshall Islands, and many other places that have been harmed by nuclear testing.

Today is the 60th birthday of my friend and partner in opposing nuclear proliferation, His Excellency Kanat Saudabayev, the Ambassador to the United States from the Republic of Kazakhstan. I do not think it is appropriate to acknowledge the fact that he is in the gallery, but I will be joining him in the gallery to congratulate him on reaching this milestone when I conclude my remarks.

It was my great pleasure in June to co-chair, at his suggestion, a public symposium in Las Vegas on the legacy and lessons of nuclear testing in Kazakhstan and Nevada. Over 100 of my constituents joined me and the Ambassador for this remarkable event, and it was with a strong sense of commitment that I submitted into the Congressional Record the Ambassador's and my joint statement of opposition to nuclear proliferation and our ongoing commitment to working for a safer world.

I salute the Ambassador, his President, and the people of Kazakhstan and look forward to working with them on eliminating the threat of nuclear testing and nuclear weapons proliferation and congratulate them for their very courageous actions.

I wholeheartedly support House Resolution 905. I commend my friend and colleague, the gentleman from American Samoa, for drafting this timely and important resolution, and I strongly urge its passage.

Mitchell B. Reiss:

Kazakhstan's commitment to principles of nonproliferation offers powerful and positive lesson for countries tempted by seductions of nuclear weapons

Kazakhstan's historic decision to renounce its nuclear arsenal and subsequent ratification of the Nonproliferation Treaty displayed true concern for the well-being of the people of Kazakhstan, and an understanding that security and economic growth could only result from full membership in the world community.

Equally as important, Kazakhstan now serves as an example to the world of a nation freely choosing to exercise restraint in the interest of humanity and to support peace and stability around the globe. In my book, *Bridled Ambition: Why Countries Constrain Their Nuclear Capabilities,* I wrote about those exceptional nations that have exercised nuclear restraint. Kazakhstan is prominent among them – the first country ever to close a nuclear test site and renounce its nuclear arsenal. Kazakhstan's commitment to the principles of nonproliferation offers a powerful and positive lesson for countries tempted by the seductions of nuclear weapons.

As the Cold War ended, Kazakhstan – with the help of the Cooperative Threat Reduction Program of Senators Nunn and Lugar – began systematically dismantling and removing the nuclear weaponry of the Soviet era. Continued close cooperation between Kazakhstan and the United States will be critical in the future as well. New threats, unimaginable at the time of Kazakhstan's independence, must be met and defeated. I commend the leaders and people of Kazakhstan on their commitment to disarmament and nonproliferation and look forward to continued U.S.-Kazakhstan friendship.

Mitchell B. Reiss is the Vice Provost for International Affairs at the College of William & Mary in Williamsburg, Virginia, and a former Director of Policy Planning at the United States Department of State. He is the author of *"Bridled Ambition: Why Countries Constrain Their Nuclear Capabilities"* and other books.

With its nuclear-free experience, Kazakhstan has not only created an effective means of political communication but successfully demonstrates its functionality, even though for now we can attest only to the beginning of this path.

The attractiveness of Kazakhstan as concept and model lies in the fact that while negating the negative (known colloquially as destruction, loss, and death), we do not talk about what the world should not be like but about what it should be, and we support our position with paradigms, guidelines, and standards tested on ourselves.

In one of my books on the historic fate of my people, I wrote that the Kazakh nation has the right not to be ashamed of a single page of its past history. And after ten years of independent development I can say that the multinational people of the Republic of Kazakhstan have nothing to be ashamed of, embarrassed by, or to justify to the world.

We did away with our nuclear fears and we freed all those who feared us from them.

We chased away illusions and made room in our land, our hearts, and our minds for realism.

We built a new non-nuclear history for the country, laying the foundation for a new narrative tradition about how to rise above a world threat. But this history is alive only when there is a circle of hearing and discussion – when the word lives on in the collective consciousness and in action.

Non-nuclear geopolitical rhetoric generously promises to become the smithy in which can be forged the materials and instruments to safeguard the security of the new world throughout the third millennium.

Excerpt from *Epicenter of Peace,* a book by
President Nursultan Nazarbayev

Kazakhstan continues to serve as a model to the global community in its leadership on disarmament and nonproliferation. I believe that it is in our nation's interest to continue to support Kazakhstan – a country whose actions have demonstrated a commitment to global stability, nonproliferation, and tolerance for ethnic and religious minorities.

U.S. Representative Brad Sherman (D-CA)

Kazakhstan has opted to become a nuclear weapon free nation thanks to the efforts of its President. President Nazarbayev is advocating something that is good for the whole world at this juncture. The world needs more presidents like him. No doubt, if all in power think and act like Kazakhstan's President, the world will be a better place today. I have great respect for his way of thinking and enforcing the concept of peaceful coexistence with other nations.

Daniel Chellaraj
Fellow, American Institute of Chemical Engineers

Not only should the story of Kazakhstan resonate throughout the world, but President Nazarbayev's brave and human approach toward a resolution of current, perilous global nuclear threats should be commended with a Nobel Peace Prize. May Kazakhstan shine as a bold example of a country which overcame tremendous and at times insurmountable difficulties to prosper in our league of nations under the guidance of one great man.

Samantha Baroni
Florida Atlantic University

Epilog

The U.S. bombings of Hiroshima and Nagasaki in 1945 brought an end to WWII and marked the arrival of the Atomic Age. The Cold War followed and an ideological struggle between the United States and the former Soviet Union ensued. The nuclear arms race was central to the Cold War and the war was widened when the U.S. began atmospheric testing in the Marshall Islands and the Soviet Union exploded its first bomb at the Semipalatinsk test site in North East Kazakhstan on August 29, 1949.

In 1991, the Soviet Union collapsed, the Cold War ended, but nuclear ambitions gained widespread appeal. As a result, one of the most pressing and vitally important subjects we now confront is the reduction of nuclear danger. Fortunately, Kazakhstan, a former Soviet Republic, stands as an example of how we can begin to address global security and peace.

After the collapse of the Soviet Union, Kazakhstan inherited a ruined economy and the world's fourth largest nuclear arsenal. This arsenal could possibly have helped to resolve the financial problems of this young nation. However, led by Nursultan Nazarbayev, the people of Kazakhstan, knowing firsthand the horrible effects of nuclear tests, made a choice to renounce nuclear weapons. In fact, immediately after achieving independence in 1991, Kazakhstan closed and sealed the world's second largest nuclear test site at Semipalatinsk at which almost 500 nuclear tests were conducted from 1949 to 1991.

Today, few know about Kazakhstan's courageous and brave decision which undoubtedly changed the course of modern history. Few know this story because Kazakhstan did not bargain and did not lobby to gain political or economic dividends from its choice. Rather, Kazakhstan, for the sake of global peace and security, consciously chose to ensure a brighter future for their children and ours.

For this reason, I believe we should speak more often of Kazakhstan's example. While I am thankful that the world is aware of the Chernobyl disaster where thousands perished, I am saddened that the world knows so little about the tragedies of Semipalatinsk and the Marshall Islands where children and the elderly have been dying for decades as a result of Cold War policies that to this day have never been set right.

In Semipalatinsk, the cumulative power of explosions from nuclear tests conducted by the former Soviet Union is believed to be equal to the power of 2,500 explosions of the type of bomb dropped on Hiroshima, Japan in 1945. More than 1.5 million people in Kazakhstan suffered as a result of these tests and a horrifying array of disease will continue to destroy the lives of hundreds of thousands and their descendants for many generations to come.

As a Pacific Islander, I have a special affinity for the people of Semipalatinsk because my people also know firsthand the horrors of nuclear testing. Bikini is one of 29 atolls and five islands that compose the Marshall Islands. These atolls are located north of the equator and are scattered over 357,000 square miles of the Pacific Ocean. Because of their location away from regular air and sea routes, these atolls were chosen to be the nuclear proving ground for the United States.

From 1946 to 1958, the United States detonated 66 nuclear weapons in the Marshall Islands including the first hydrogen bomb, or Bravo shot, which was 1,000 times more powerful than the bomb dropped on Hiroshima. Acknowledged as the greatest nuclear explosion ever detonated, the Bravo shot vaporized six islands and created a mushroom cloud 25 miles in diameter.

It has been said that if one were to calculate the net yield of the tests conducted in the Marshall Islands, it would be equivalent to the detonation of 1.7 Hiroshima bombs every day for twelve years. Like the people of Semipalatinsk, the people of the Marshall Islands still suffer as a result of these tests.

Again, while their story remains mostly untold, hundreds of thousands of Kazakhs and thousands of Marshallese still suffer as a result of the historic contributions they made in bringing an end to the Cold War. This is why I welcome and express my appreciation to the organizers of the important conference entitled Kazakhstan: Strengthening International Cooperation for Peace and Security. I am pleased to acknowledge that it has become a logical extension of the symposium held in Washington D.C. in December of 2003 entitled *Kazakhstan: Reducing Nuclear Danger, Increasing Global Security.*

As a direct result of the 2003 conference and the vision and leadership of His Excellency Kanat Saudabayev, Ambassador of the Republic of Kazakhstan, who has worked tirelessly to bring these issues to the attention of the U.S. Congress, I became aware of the magnitude of the problem of Semipalatinsk and, in response, initiated legislation calling for the creation of a joint working group to assist the people of Semipalatinsk. My colleagues supported this effort and the U.S. House of Representatives passed this legislation on July 16, 2004.

In August 2004, I thought it was my duty as a Member of Congress and as a Pacific Islander serving as the Ranking Member of the International Relations Subcommittee on Asia and the Pacific, to visit the Semipalatinsk test site. During my visit, I was amazed to learn that I was the first American legislator to set foot on ground zero.

Considering the courageous decision made by the people and the President of Kazakhstan to seal and close this site so that you and I and generations to come may live in peace, I believe we have a moral responsibility to visit this region more frequently lest we forget the sacrifices made to preserve international peace. In remembering, I believe we have an obligation to look beyond figures and statistics.

This is why I personally visited with the victims of nuclear testing. I met many of them in poorly equipped hospitals in Semipalatinsk. In their eyes, I saw a flicker of hope. In the eyes of their children, I saw a better future. But without our help, neither is possible.

The time has come for us to live up to the hopes and prayers of our brothers and sisters in Semipalatinsk. Their suffering is not just Kazakhstan's responsibility. It is our duty as a world community to bear their burdens. And this was the subject of my conversation with President Nazarbayev whose decision to shut down the Semipalatinsk test site in spite of threats from the Kremlin eloquently characterizes him as a true leader to whom we owe much.

In 2005, we celebrated the 10th anniversary of Kazakhstan's nuclear free status. In April of the same year, the U.S. Senate unanimously passed Resolution 122, recognizing the historic efforts of the Republic of Kazakhstan to reduce the threat of weapons of mass destruction, and celebrating the 10th anniversary of the removal of all nuclear weapons from the territory of Kazakhstan. On this occasion, my colleagues and I also sent a letter to President Nazarbayev thanking Kazakhstan for its contribution to nonproliferation and global security. Finally, in July 2006, the United States House of Representatives unanimously passed the historic Resolution 905, congratulating Kazakhstan on the 15th anniversary of the closure of the world's second largest nuclear test site in the Semipalatinsk region of Kazakhstan and for its efforts on the nonproliferation of weapons of mass destruction.

As important as these recognitions are, I believe the international community should also take notice. While I am pleased that the 2005 Nobel Peace Prize was awarded to Dr. Mohamed ElBaradei, Director General of the International Atomic Energy Agency, and the IAEA, I believe President Nazarbayev should also receive the Nobel Peace Prize for dismantling the world's fourth largest nuclear arsenal and closing and sealing the Semipalatinsk test site.

I also believe the people of Kazakhstan and the Marshall Islands should be recognized for the historic contributions they have made to reduce nuclear danger and strengthen global security. It is only fitting and fair that their contributions should be acknowledged and I am hopeful that their story will be told.

> Eni F.H. Faleomavaega
> Member of the United States Congress
> (D-American Samoa)

Copyright Information

208